The Health and Medical Care
of African-Americans

Volume V

Wornie L. Reed

with

**William Darity, Sr.
Stanford Roman
Claudia Baquet
Noma L. Roberson**

**William Monroe Trotter Institute
University of Massachusetts at Boston**

1992

Table of Contents

PREFACE

In the Spring of 1987 the William Monroe Trotter Institute at the University of Massachusetts at Boston initiated a project entitled, "The Assessment of the Status of African-Americans." Thirty-five scholars were organized into study groups, one for each of six topics: education; employment, income, and occupations; political participation and the administration of justice; social and cultural change; health status and medical care; and the family. The study groups were established to analyze the status of African-Americans in each of the topical areas in anticipation of the results and analyses of the National Research Council's Study Committee on the Status of Black Americans. We wanted to have the widest possible discussion of the present condition of blacks and the social policy implications of that condition.

The multidisciplinary group of scholars comprising the study groups included persons from all sections of the country and from varied settings–private and public universities, historically black universities, and private agencies. A list of these scholars by study group is given in the Appendix. Each of the study groups met and drafted an agenda for examining significant issues under their respective topics. Members chose issues from this agenda within their areas of expertise and identified other scholars who had written extensively on other issues on the agenda. These other scholars made a variety of contributions, including original papers, reprints, notes and materials, and/or substantial commentaries on draft documents.

Despite the pressures of limited time and limited financial support for this work, six volumes were produced:

Volume I: *Summary*
Volume II: *Research on the African-American Family: A Holistic Perspective*
Volume III: *The Education of African-Americans*
Volume IV: *Social, Political, and Economic Issues in Black America*
Volume V: *The Health and Medical Care of African-Americans*
Volume VI: *Critiques of NRC Study*, A Common Destiny: Blacks and
             American Society

Each of the study groups developed its own conclusion and policy recommendations.

In addition to study group members and other contributors, we are indebted to a number of individuals for the production of this study. We owe thanks to Phillip Hallen and the Maurice Falk Foundation for underwriting the costs of producing these volumes. Special thanks are also offered to the following persons: our editors, Suzanne Baker and Linda Kluz, and our production staff, Eva Hendricks and Gemima Remy.

During production of this volume I relocated from the University of Massachusetts at Boston to Cleveland State University. Special thanks are given to Dr. James Jennings, Interim Director of the Trotter Institute, for supporting the completion of this volume.

Wornie L. Reed

1

Health Status and Sociodemographic Context

The consequences and the legacy of racism and racial discrimination are serious matters. These issues are often thought of in terms of attitudes and inconveniences. However, institutional racism affects the life chances of African-Americans–i.e., how well and how long they live. Racial disadvantages in the United States–especially as they relate to blacks in comparison to whites–are nowhere more telling and perhaps more significant than in mortality rates and life expectancy. Blacks do not live as long as whites.

The seriousness of the health status of African-Americans in urban areas was shown in a recent study that compared the mortality rates of blacks in Harlem to those of whites in New York City (McCord and Freeman, 1990). Blacks were several times more likely to die than whites. In fact, the life expectancy of black males in the central Harlem district was found to be lower than that of males in Bangladesh; and Bangladesh is categorized by the World Bank as one of the poorest countries in the world.

The McCord and Freeman study also profiled the socioeconomic conditions in Harlem: Harlem is 96% black, and 41% of the population lives below the poverty line. It is becoming increasingly apparent that health problems confronting the black community are directly related to socioeconomic conditions. Before providing an overview of the health status of African-Americans we will provide a brief sociodemographic context.

Sociodemographic Context

In 1987 blacks were more than three times as likely to be below the poverty level as whites, a situation that has persisted for several decades (table 1-1). Children and the elderly are more likely than other age groups to be below the poverty level for whites as well as blacks; however, the same racial ratio obtains–black children and older persons are more than three times as likely to be below the poverty level than white children and older persons (U.S. Department of Health and Human Services, 1990).

High school graduation rates are a significant indicator of actual as well as potential socioeconomic status. Therefore, the upward trend of this statistic since 1970 is a positive development–both black males and black females had increases in high school graduation rates. However, in 1986 the non-high school graduation rate for blacks was still significantly higher than that for whites (See table 1-2).

Table 1-1

Percent of Persons Below the Poverty Level, by Race:
United States, Selected Years, 1960-1987

Year	Race	
	White	Black
1960	17.8	55.9a
1962	16.4	55.8a
1964	14.9	49.6a
1966	11.3	41.8
1968	10.0	34.7
1970	9.4	33.5
1972	9.0	33.3
1974	8.6	30.3
1976	9.1	31.1
1978	8.7	30.6
1980	10.2	32.5
1982	12.0	35.6
1984	11.5	33.8
1986	11.0	33.1
1987	10.5	33.1

aPrior to 1966, category includes blacks and other races.

Source: U.S. Department of Health and Human Services. (1990). *Health Status of the Disadvantaged–Chartbook 1990*. DHHS Pub. No. (HRSA) HRS-P-DV 90-1. Washington, DC: U.S. Government Printing Office.

Table 1-2

Persons Not Enrolled in School and Not High School Graduates,
by Age, Race, and Sex: United States, Selected Years, 1970-1986

Characteristic by Year	Age			
	Total 16-24 yrs.	16-17 yrs.	18-19 yrs.	20-24 yrs.
	(Percent)			
1970				
White male	12.2	6.3	13.3	14.8
White female	14.1	8.4	14.8	16.3
Black male	29.4	13.1	36.4	35.4
Black female	26.6	12.4	26.6	35.5
1972				
White male	13.0	7.8	13.5	15.3
White female	14.2	9.6	13.2	16.6
Black male	22.3	9.4	27.1	27.2
Black female	20.8	7.6	21.0	27.3
1974				
White male	13.4	9.4	17.4	13.6
White female	13.1	9.1	13.9	14.5
Black male	20.1	8.3	26.9	23.6
Black female	22.3	12.6	20.2	27.7
1976				
White male	13.2	7.6	17.1	14.1
White female	13.3	9.1	15.4	14.1
Black male	21.2	8.1	19.3	29.6
Black female	19.7	10.8	20.7	23.5
1978				
White male	13.9	8.6	17.0	14.9
White female	12.8	9.1	14.8	13.5
Black male	19.4	6.9	23.8	24.3
Black female	20.0	8.4	20.3	25.1
1980				
White male	14.2	9.3	16.1	15.5
White female	12.3	9.2	13.8	12.9
Black male	21.1	7.1	22.7	27.6
Black female	17.9	6.7	19.9	21.7

Table 1-2
(continued)

Persons Not Enrolled in School and Not High School Graduates,
by Age, Race, and Sex: United States, Selected Years, 1970-1986

Characteristic by Year	Age			
	Total 16-24 yrs.	16-17 yrs.	18-19 yrs.	20-24 yrs.
1982				
White male	13.6	7.2	16.6	14.7
White female	12.7	8.0	14.9	13.5
Black male	21.1	6.4	26.4	25.3
Black female	16.0	5.5	18.1	19.1
1984				
White male	13.5	7.4	15.8	14.9
White female	11.8	6.9	14.0	12.6
Black male	16.7	5.5	19.7	20.1
Black female	14.5	4.9	14.4	18.0
1986				
White male	12.9	6.9	12.8	15.3
White female	11.1	6.0	11.0	12.9
Black male	14.9	4.7	14.6	19.6
Black female	13.4	4.7	15.2	16.0

Source: U.S. Department of Health and Human Services. (1990). *Health Status of the Disadvantaged–Chartbook 1990*. DHHS Pub. No. (HRSA) HRS-P-DV 90-1. Washington, DC: U.S. Government Printing Office.

Table 1-3 reveals a great deal about race, education, and poverty status of families. First, it shows that black families are more than three-and-one-half times as likely to be in poverty as are white families. It also shows that family heads of black origin were more likely than whites in every educational category to be below the poverty level. The difference is greatest among those with some college education, thus indicating that although the education gap is closing, the poverty gap is not.

Between 1982 and 1987 median family income increased for white and black families. However, there remained a substantial difference between races, as black families earned only about 56% of the income of white families in both 1982 and 1987 (table 1-4).

Table 1-5 illustrates the socioeconomic impact of an increasing trend: the growth of single-parent female-headed households. Married-couple families are several times less likely to be in poverty than male or female householders with no spouse present, although female householders with no husband present are more than twice as likely to be in poverty as are single-parent males. More than one-half of the black female-headed households were below the poverty level in 1987, compared to slightly more than one-fourth of households headed by white females. An additional point not to be overlooked is the fact that black married-couple families are more than twice as likely to be in poverty as white married-couple families (table 1-5).

Health Status

As mentioned above black Americans do not live as long as white Americans. In fact, in 1986 life expectancy for blacks declined for the second year in a row, the first back-to-back annual decline in this century. Although the expected life span of whites increased steadily during the 1980s, the life expectancy for black males began declining in 1985. The life expectancy for black females dropped in 1985 as well but began to exceed previous estimates again in 1988 (table 1-6).

African-Americans are at a higher risk of death than whites throughout the life span, except at very advanced ages. For infants and for adults between the ages 25 and 45 blacks have significantly more than twice the risk of death (see table 1-7). One means of expressing these racial differentials in mortality is the "excess deaths" index. This index expresses the difference between the number of deaths actually observed among blacks and the number of deaths that would have occurred if blacks had experienced the same death rates for each age and sex as the white population. During the period 1979 to 1981, for black males and females combined, excess deaths accounted for 47% of the total annual deaths of blacks 45 years old or less, and for 42% of deaths in blacks aged 70 years or less (table 1-8).

Table 1-8 also indicates the six leading causes of excess deaths among blacks aged 70 years or less. In order from greatest to least they are heart disease and stroke, homicide and accidents, cancer, infant mortality, cirrhosis, and diabetes.

Table 1-3

Educational Attainment of Family Head by Poverty Status, by Race: United States, 1987

Level of Education	All Races Below Poverty Level			White Below Poverty Level			Black Below Poverty Level		
	Total	Number	% Total	Total	Number	% Total	Total	Number	% Total
Total, all families	65,133	7,059	10.8	56,044	4,592	8.2	7,177	2,149	29.9
Total, 25 yrs. and over	62,207	6,196	10.0	53,696	4,034	7.5	6,674	1,865	27.9
Elementary: total	7,499	1,759	23.5	6,057	1,230	20.3	1,203	432	35.9
Less than 8 years	4,264	1,207	28.3	3,259	827	25.4	821	299	36.4
8 years	3,235	552	17.1	2,798	403	14.4	382	133	34.9
High school: total	30,420	3,538	11.6	26,056	2,187	8.4	3,773	1,241	32.9
1-3 years	7,475	1,406	18.8	6,036	810	13.4	1,306	556	42.6
4 years	22,945	2,132	9.3	20,020	1,377	6.9	2,467	685	27.8
College: 1 year or more	24,288	899	3.7	21,583	617	2.9	1,699	191	11.2

Source: U.S. Department of Health and Human Services. (1990). *Health Status of the Disadvantaged–Chartbook 1990*. Washington, DC: U.S. Government Printing Office. DHHS Pub. No. (HRSA) HRS-P-DV 90-1.

Table 1-4

Median Income of Families, by Race of Head of Household:
United States, Selected Years, 1960-1987

Year	All Races	White	Black
1960a	$18,317	$19,018	$10,528
1965a	21,283	22,183	12,216
1970	24,528	25,445	15,608
1975	24,604	25,589	15,744
1978	26,099	27,176	16,096
1979b	26,047	27,180	15,391
1980	24,626	25,658	14,846
1982	23,433	24,603	13,598
1984	26,433	27,686	15,432
1986	29,458	30,809	17,604
1987	30,853	32,274	18,098

aFor 1960 and 1965, data for blacks includes blacks plus other races.
bBeginning with 1979 based on household concept and restricted to primary families.

Source: U.S. Department of Health and Human Services. (1990). *Health Status of the Disadvantaged–Chartbook 1990*. DHHS Pub. No. (HRSA) HRS-P-DV 90-1. Washington, DC: U.S. Government Printing Office.

Table 1-5

Number of Families and Poverty Rate for Families, by Sex
and Race of Householder: United States, 1987

Sex of Householder	Number of Families Below Poverty Rate (in 1,000s)		Family Poverty Rate[a]	
	White	Black	White	Black
All families	4,592	2,149	8.2	29.9
Married-couple families:	2,440	454	5.2	12.3
Male householder	2,260	404	5.1	12.6
Female householder	180	50	7.3	10.3
Male householder, No wife present	223	102	10.3	24.3
Female householder, No husband present	1,930	1,593	26.7	51.8

[a]Families below poverty level as a percent of all families.

Source: U.S. Department of Health and Human Services. (1990). *Health Status of the Disadvantaged–Chartbook 1990*. DHHS Pub. No. (HRSA) HRS-P-DV 90-1. Washington, DC: U.S. Government Printing Office.

Table 1-6

Life Expectancy at Birth, by Race and Sex: United States, Selected Years, 1970-1988

Year	White		Black	
	Male	Female	Male	Female
1970	68.0	75.6	60.0	68.3
1975	69.5	77.3	62.4	71.3
1980	70.7	78.1	63.8	72.5
1981	71.1	78.4	64.5	73.2
1982	71.5	78.7	65.1	73.7
1983	71.7	78.7	65.4	73.6
1984	71.8	78.7	65.6	73.7
1985	71.9	78.7	65.3	73.5
1986	72.0	78.8	65.2	73.5
1987	72.2	78.9	65.2	73.6
1988	72.1	78.9	65.1	73.8

Source: U.S. Bureau of the Census, *Statistical Abstract of the United States 1989*. Washington, DC: U.S. Department of Commerce.

Table 1-7

Relative Risk of Mortality for Blacks Compared with
Whites for All Causes of Death: United States, 1979-81

Age	Blacks	
	Male	Female
Total (all ages)	1.05	.90
Under 1	2.10	2.20
1-4	1.67	1.71
5-14	1.35	1.33
15-24	1.25	1.27
25-34	2.37	2.29
35-44	2.67	2.34
45-54	2.11	2.06
55-64	1.66	1.78
65-74	1.27	1.47
75-84	1.04	1.15
85 +	0.84	0.82

Source: U.S. Department of Health and Human Services. (1985). *Report of the Secretary's Task Force on Black and Minority Health–Volume II Crosscutting Issues in Minority Health.* Washington, DC: U.S. Government Printing Office.

Table 1-8

Average Annual Total and Excess Deaths in Blacks for
Selected Causes of Mortality: United States, 1979-1981

Causes of Excess Death	Excess Deaths Males and Females Cumulative to Age 45		Excess Deaths Males an Females Cumulative to Age 70	
	Number	Percent	Number	Percent
Heart disease and stroke	3,312	14.4	18,181	30.8
Homicide and accidents	8,041	35.1	10,909	18.5
Cancer	874	3.8	8,118	13.8
Infant mortality	6,178	26.9	6,178	10.5
Cirrhosis	1,121	4.9	2,154	3.7
Diabetes	223	1.0	1,850	3.1
Subtotal	19,749	86.1	47,390	80.4
All other causes	3,187	13.9	11,552	19.6
Total excess deaths	22,936	100.0	58,942	100.0
Total deaths, all causes	48,323		138,635	
Ratio of excess deaths to total deaths	47.4%		42.5%	
Percent contribution of six causes to excess death	86.1%		80.4%	

Source: U.S. Department of Health and Human Services. (1985). *Report of the Secretary's Task Force on Black and Minority Health–Volume II Crosscutting Issues in Minority Health.* Washington, DC: U.S. Government Printing Office.

These six causes account for 80.4% of excess deaths. For blacks aged 45 and under homicide and accidents are the number one cause of death with infant mortality second.

Another measure used to illustrate racial differentials in mortality is "person-years of life lost," which incorporates the impact of the age of death on black/white differences. Statistics for the U.S. government indicate that among black men, over 900,000 years of life before age 70 are lost each year in excess of the person-years lost by white men. Among black females nearly 600,000 excess person-years are lost annually in excess of the loss among white females (U. S. Department of Health and Human Services, 1986). If blacks had the same death rate as whites, 59,000 black deaths a year would not occur.

Between 1950 and 1980 there was a widening of the gap in mortality rates between blacks and whites. For example, in 1950 the adjusted death rate per 100,000 residents for all causes was 841.5, and in 1980 it was 585.8, a 30.4% decrease for the overall population. In 1950 the rate for black males was 1,373 per 100,000 black residents and for white males it was 963.1, a difference of 410 per 100,00 persons. The differential deficit ratio (the extent to which the black rate exceeds the white rate) was 42.6%. In 1980 the death rate for black males was 1,112.8 per 100,000 persons and for white males 745.3 per 100,000, a difference of 367.5. Even though the difference had decreased, the differential deficit ratio of deaths from all causes between black males and white males had increased from 42.6% to 49.3%. This was an increase of 6.7% deficit over the 30-year period (National Center for Health Statistics, 1990).

Among females, however, the differential deficit ratio decreased between 1950 and 1980. For black females the death rate for all causes in 1950 was 1,106 per 100,000. For white females it was 650 per 100,000, a difference of 456.7 and a differential deficit ratio of 70.3%. By 1980 this gap had decreased to 56.3%, a decrease of 17.1% (National Center for Health Statistics, 1990).

Selected Diseases

Table 1-9 shows age-adjusted death rates for whites and blacks for four selected chronic diseases: diseases of the heart, cerebrovascular diseases, malignant neoplasms (cancers), and diabetes mellitus. Although age-adjusted death rates for these diseases have declined for all races since 1960, blacks continue to have much higher rates than whites for these four diseases. In addition, among black males the death rate for diabetes actually increased in the period 1960-1987.

As may be inferred from the data presented above, blacks not only do not live as long as whites, they do not live as healthily. The disproportionate death rates are indicative of disadvantages in health status. Blacks are more at risk for ill health from several of the major chronic diseases.

Table 1-9

Age-Adjusted Death Rates for Selected Chronic Disease Conditions: United States, Selected Years, 1960-1987

Selected Chronic Disease	Selected Years							
	1960	1970	1980	1982	1984	1986	1987
All races: rate per 100,000 population							
Disease of the heart	286.2	253.6	202.0	190.5	183.6	175.0	169.6
Cerebrovascular disease	79.7	6.3	40.8	35.8	33.4	31.0	30.3
Malignant neoplasms	125.8	29.9	132.8	132.5	133.5	133.2	132.9
Diabetes mellitus	13.6	14.1	10.1	9.6	9.5	9.6	9.8
White males: rate per 100,000 white male population							
Disease of the heart	375.4	347.6	277.5	262.1	249.5	234.8	225.9
Cerebrovascular disease	80.3	8.8	41.9	36.6	33.9	31.1	30.3
Malignant neoplasms	141.6	54.3	160.5	159.4	159.0	158.8	158.4
Diabetes mellitus	11.6	12.7	9.5	9.2	9.0	9.1	9.5
White females: rate per 100,000 white female population							
Disease of the heart	197.1	167.8	134.6	127.4	124.0	119.0	116.3
Cerebrovascular disease	68.7	6.2	35.2	31.0	28.9	27.1	26.3
Malignant neoplasms	109.5	107.6	107.7	108.2	109.9	110.1	109.7
Diabetes mellitus	13.7	12.8	8.7	8.3	8.0	8.1	8.1
Black males: rate per 100,000 black male population							
Disease of the heart	381.2	375.9	327.3	309.4	300.1	294.3	287.1
Cerebrovascular disease	141.2	24.2	77.5	68.9	62.8	58.9	57.1
Malignant neoplasms	158.5	98.0	229.9	235.2	234.9	229.0	227.9
Diabetes mellitus	16.2	21.2	17.7	16.1	17.6	17.9	18.3
White females: rate per 100,000 white female population							
Disease of the heart	292.6	251.7	201.1	186.3	186.6	185.1	180.8
Cerebrovascular disease	139.5	107.9	61.7	54.7	51.8	47.6	46.7
Malignant neoplasms	127.8	23.5	129.7	128.7	131.0	132.1	132.0
Diabetes mellitus	27.3	30.9	22.1	19.8	20.5	21.4	21.3

Source: U.S. Department of Health and Human Services. (1990). *Health Status of the Disadvantaged–Chartbook 1990.* DHHS Pub. No. (HRSA) HRS-P-DV 90-1. Washington, DC: U.S. Government Printing Office.

Table 1-10

Relative Risk of Morbidity for Blacks Compared with Whites,
Selected Conditions by Age and Gender: United States, 1978-80

Age	Hypertension Males	Hypertension Females	Diseases of the Circulatory System Males	Diseases of the Circulatory System Females	Diabetes Males	Diabetes Females	Arthritis Males	Arthritis Females
1-14	4.03	3.73	1.60	2.33	0.22	1.15	0.78	0.36
15-24	3.37	3.76	1.88	2.31	0.39	0.68	0.73	0.36
24-44	2.73	4.54	1.86	2.91	0.23	2.16	0.65	1.16
45-64	2.67	3.20	1.41	2.31	2.43	2.82	1.71	1.64
65-69	2.53	2.31	1.40	1.68	2.30	2.87	1.57	1.40
70+	2.39	2.22	1.33	1.62	1.85	2.22	1.71	1.54

Source: U.S. Department of Health and Human Services. (1985). *Report of the Secretary's Task Force on Black and Minority Health–Volume II Crosscutting Issues in Minority Health.* Washington, DC: U.S. Government Office.

Chronic disease conditions are the leading causes of both morbidity and mortality in the United States today. The three leading causes of death are chronic diseases–diseases of the heart, malignant neoplasms, and cerebrovascular diseases– and blacks have higher death rates for each of these diseases (see table 1-9). These three diseases are also responsible for an estimated 15% of the national daily limitations of activity due to chronic conditions (U.S. Department of Health and Human Services, 1985).

Cardiovascular diseases are the major diseases in the United States today, as they are the cause of almost half of all deaths (U.S. Department of Health and Human Services, 1985). This disease category comprises all diseases of the heart and blood vessels. It includes diseases of the heart, hypertension, cerebrovascular diseases (including stroke), arteriosclerosis, and other diseases of the arteries. Most of these diseases are subsumed under the heading, "diseases of the circulatory system," in table 1-10. This table indicates the extent to which blacks suffer in excess from these diseases–from a low of one-and-one-third times whites among males over 70 years of age to nearly three times for females age 24 to 44. And for the particular disease hypertension the black excess is much higher.

Blacks also have excess morbidity (in comparison to whites) for diabetes and arthritis (table 1-10). Arthritis is the cause of a great deal of disability, while diabetes is a major cause of death.

Summary

For many health status indicators the rates are improving for blacks as well as whites. However, a racial gap still remains, and in some instances the gap has increased over the past decade or two. In a search for relevant factors associated with these trends we will examine several health issues in the following chapters.

References

Cord, C. & Freeman, H. (1990). Excess Mortality in Harlem. *New England Journal of Medicine, 322*: 173-177.

National Center for Health Statistics. (1990). *Health United States, 1989.* Hyattsville, MD: Public Health Service.

U.S. Department of Health and Human Services. (1986). *Report of the Secretary's Task Force of Black and Minority Health, Vol. 2: Crosscutting Issues in Minority Health.* Washington, DC: U.S. Government Printing Office.

U.S. Department of Health and Human Services. (1985). *Health Status of Minorities and Low Income Groups*. DHHS Pub. No. (HRSA) HRS-P-DV 85-1. Washington, DC: U.S. Government Printing Office.

U.S. Department of Health and Human Services. (1990). *Health Status of the Disadvanted–Chartbook 1990*. DHHS Pub. No. (HRSA) HRS-P-DV 90-1. Washington, DC: U.S. Government Printing Office.

2

Adverse Birth Outcomes: Infant Mortality, Low Birth Weight, and Maternal Deaths

A nation's health is reflected in the mortality and morbidity status of its children. Indices such as infant mortality, low birth weight, and maternal mortality reflect the general welfare of a population group. In this chapter we will examine the trends in these adverse birth outcomes among African-Americans and make comparisons between white and black Americans. This examination suggests quite strongly that in comparison to whites and to some population groups in other countries black Americans do not benefit as well as should be expected given the wealth of American society. Factors associated with the reduction of adverse birth outcomes are also discussed.

Infant Mortality

One of the most critical indices used nationally and internationally to interpret the health status of a population group is the infant mortality rate–the number of children dying before one year of age per 1,000 live births. This index provides clues about the health care situation, the income level, the housing situation, and the overall socioeconomic condition of a population group, as well as the nutritional status of the mothers in this group. In other words, a high infant mortality rate is indicative of the overall deprivation that impinges on the health of a population group.

In the United States the infant mortality rate (IMR) has declined throughout this century for the overall population, and it has been decreasing among blacks as well as whites. However, in recent years the gap between the IMR for the black population and the IMR for the white population has been widening, that is, the infant mortality rate for blacks has not been declining as rapidly as the white rate. Thus, the gap or difference between the rates for blacks and the rates for whites is increasing. In other words, the "differential deficit ratio," the percentage required for blacks to catch up if the overall infant mortality ratio for whites stood still, was wider in the 1980s than it was in the 1950s. As can be seen in table 2-1, in 1950 the overall IMR was 29.2 per 1,000 live births–26.8 for white Americans and 43.9 for the black Americans. The difference was 17.1, which is a differential deficit ratio of .638 or 63.8%. Although there was a decrease in the infant mortality rate over the next 15 years, the differential deficit ratio between blacks and whites continued to increase. For example, in 1965 the IMR was 41.7 for black Americans and 21.5 for white Americans, for a differential deficit ratio of .940 or 94%.

Table 2-1

Infant Mortality Rates, by Race, with Differential Deficit Ratio, 1950-1987
(Rate per 1,000 Live Births)

| Year | Total | White | All Other | | Difference Between Blacks and Whites | Differential Deficit Ratio |
			Nonwhite	Black		
1950	29.2	26.8	44.5	43.9	17.1	.638 or 63.8%
1955	26.4	23.6	42.8	43.1	19.5	.826 or 82.6%
1960	26.0	22.9	43.2	44.3	21.4	.934 or 93.4%
1965	24.7	21.5	40.3	41.7	20.2	.940 or 94.0%
1970	20.0	17.8	30.9	32.6	14.8	.831 or 83.1%
1971	19.1	17.1	28.5	30.3	13.2	.772 or 77.2%
1972	18.5	16.4	27.2	29.6	13.2	.805 or 80.5%
1973	17.7	15.8	26.2	28.1	12.3	.778 or 77.8%
1974	16.7	14.8	24.9	26.8	12.0	.811 or 81.1%
1975	16.1	14.2	24.2	26.2	12.0	.845 or 84.5%
1980	12.5	11.41	–	21.8	9.3	.744 or 74.4%
1982	11.2	9.92	–	19.3	10.4	.949 or 94.9%
1983	11.2	9.73	–	19.2	9.5	.979 or 97.9%
1984	10.8	9.4	–	18.4	9.0	.957 or 95.7%
1985	10.6	9.3	–	17.9	9.3	.957 or 95.7%
1986	10.4	8.9	–	18.0	9.1	1.022 or 102.2%
1987	10.1	8.6	–	17.9	9.3	1.081 or 108.1%

Source: National Center for Health Statistics. (1982, December). *Health, United States, 1982*. DHHS Pub. No. (PHS) 83-1232. Public Health Services. Washington, DC: U.S. Government Printing Office; National Center for Health Statistics. (1990). *Health, United States, 1989*. DHHS Pub. No. 90-1232. Hyattsville, MD: Public Health Service.

A closing of the gap occurred by 1970 when the IMR was 32.6 for blacks and 17.8 for whites with a differential deficit ratio of .831 or 83.1%. Although a continuous decrease in the IMR for both races occurred after 1970, by 1975 the gap began widening again with a differential deficit ratio of .845 or 84.5%. In 1980 the differential deficit ratio reached an all time low for the decade at 74.4%, but by 1982 the ratio had reached .949 or 94.9%, the highest in the last 30 years. More recent data present on ominous situation: the ratio increased to 108.1% in 1987.

In 1987 the five leading causes of infant death were, in order: congenital anomalies, sudden infant death syndrome, disorders relating to short gestation and unspecified low birth weight, respiratory distress syndrome, and newborns affected by maternal complications of pregnancy. Except for congenital anomalies, the risk for each of these was substantially higher for black infants than for white infants, with the largest discrepancy in "disorders relating to short gestation and unspecified low birth weight" (National Center for Health Statistics, 1990). Black infant mortality for this cause was 3.4 times that of white infants.

Infant mortality rates for all races have declined substantially since 1950; however, as shown in table 2-2, the rates for black Americans have declined slower than other races. At 19.2 in 1983 the infant mortality rate for blacks was the highest of all racial groups. The lowest infant mortality was among Japanese-Americans, at 4.3. It was 6.5 for Chinese-Americans, 9.7 for white Americans, 10.7 for native Americans, and 3.0 for all other races. The steady decline in the total IMR experienced during the twentieth century is due to reductions in deaths from infectious diseases as a result of improvements in public health sanitation, better nutrition and living conditions, widespread immunization, and improved access to medical care. However, in the 1980s the ratio of black-to-white (the differential deficit ratio) infant death rates began to increase as the black rate declined more slowly than the white rate. In 1983 a black infant in Chicago, Cleveland, or Detroit was more likely to die in the first year of life than an infant born in Costa Rica (Kramer, 1988), indicating that the environment in which many black children in this country are reared more closely resembles that of Third World countries than the affluent United States.

The infant mortality rate for native Americans has declined much more rapidly than has the rate for African-Americans. In 1950 the IMR of native Americans was nearly twice that of African-Americans; and in 1983 it was only slightly more than one-half that of African-Americans. This raises the question of how infant mortality among native Americans can be reduced so much more substantially than among African-Americans when their demographic profiles are similar. Kramer (1988) argues that the most apparent difference between African-Americans and native Americans is that native Americans enrolled in federally recognized tribes and living near an Indian Health Service facility have access to free health services that are fairly comprehensive. They can seek services within that system without the stigma of financial means tests or the fear of being turned away because the provider does not wish to serve poor clients at below regular reimbursement rates.

Table 2-2

Infant Mortality Rates, by Race, with Percentage Decrease, 1950-1983
(Rate per 1,000 Live Births)

Year	All Races	White	Black	Native Americans	Chinese-American	Japanese-American	Other Races
1950	29.2	26.8	43.9	82.1	19.3	19.1	27.9
1955	26.4	23.6	43.1	59.7	18.1	10.9	17.6
1960	26.0	22.9	44.3	49.3	14.7	15.3	23.5
1965	24.7	21.5	41.7	NA	9.0	10.0	NA
1970	20.0	17.8	32.7	22.0	8.4	10.5	14.8
1975	16.1	14.2	26.1	17.8	4.4	6.9	9.8
1978	13.8	12.0	23.1	13.7	6.3	6.5	8.5
1980	12.6	11.0	21.4	13.2	5.3	4.5	2.8
1983	11.6	9.7	19.2	10.7	6.5	4.3	3.0

Percentage Decrease

1950-1978	112%	123%	90.4%	499%	206%	193%	228%
1950-1983	152%	176%	128%	667%	197%	344%	830%

Source: U.S. Department of Health and Human Services. (1986). *Health Status of the Disadvantaged, Chartbook 1986.* DHHS Pub. No. (HRSA) HRS-P-DV86-2. Washington, DC: U.S. Government Printing Office.

In the general population there has been a reduction in the provision of maternal and child health services. A study by the Children's Defense Fund (1986) found that in 1985 Medicaid reached only 46% of poor and near-poor families compared to 65% in 1969. In that same year 42 states served fewer than half of all those eligible for Women, Infants and Children (WIC) nutritional supplements. The Children's Defense Fund (1986) explained how these cutbacks and problems in the economy (recessions, etc.) combined to affect the health of black children:

> The dramatic upswing in childhood poverty from 1979 to 1983 and the downswing in vital public health, nutrition, and family support services from 1981 to 1983 have been accompanied by a marked slowdown in the decline of overall and neonatal infant mortality, a nationwide rise in postneonatal infant mortality, an increase in the percentage of low birth weight babies and in women receiving late or no prenatal care, and the widest disparity in more than four decades between the infant mortality rates of blacks and whites. (p. xi)

One argument given as the reason native American programs did not have similar cuts is that this population group constitutes such a small proportion of the total U.S. population that only relatively small savings could be had by cutting them, and at the same time there were substantial political or conscience-soothing benefits to maintaining them (Kramer, 1988).

Low Birth Weight Infants

Low birth weight infants–those weighing less than 2,500 grams (5 pounds 8 ounces)–are at greater risk not only of dying during the first year of life but also of developing long-term disabilities. In other words, some of the low birth weight infants die, but many more live and suffer various health and neurological effects as a result of their low birth weight.

Of all infants who die, about 60% are of low birth weight. Of these, about 40% are of very low birth weight (weighing less than 1,500 grams at birth). Table 2-3 shows that 12.6 % of black babies were low weight in the 1985-87 period, compared to 5.7% of whites. Blacks have an even greater proportion of very low birth weight babies–2.7 for blacks versus 0.9 for whites. Some of the factors associated with low birth weight and other major causes of infant death are lack of prenatal care by expectant mothers (see discussion of prenatal care below), maternal smoking, alcohol and drug use, age, and socioeconomic background of the mother.

Appropriate nutrition and low usage of alcohol and cigarettes are some of the key preventive measures that are suggested for the improvement of the birth status of black infants. Other proposals include reaching more black women with appropriate and timely prenatal care and educating men as well as women about the relationship between successful pregnancy outcomes and healthful lifestyles.

Maternal Mortality

Maternal mortality–death from complications of pregnancy–is yet another problem of pregnancy and childbirth that disproportionately affects blacks. Maternal deaths result from a number of causes, including pre-existing health problems aggravated by the pregnancy, pregnancy-related condition such as pre-eclampsia, and complications of labor and delivery. For blacks the main causes of maternal mortality are ectopic pregnancy, eclampsia, toxemia, and pre-eclampsia, in that order (Hughes, Johnson, Rosenbaum, Butler, & Simons, 1988). There has been a fairly steady decline in maternal mortality over the past four decades among blacks as well as whites (see table 2-4). Yet black women are three to four times more likely to die from complications of childbirth than white women. Black women are seven times more likely than white women to die as a result of anemia and five to nine times more likely to die from anesthetic-related causes during uncomplicated deliveries. Thus, much of the black excess maternal mortality arises from preventable causes, in addition to reduced access to care (Hughes et al., 1988).

Some researches argue that less access to, and less utilization of, obstetric care by black and other minority women are factors in the higher maternal mortality rates of these groups (Hughes et al., 1988). A lifetime of poor access to needed medical care adversely affects prepregnancy health, which in turn adversely affects pregnancy and pregnancy outcome. Suggested preventive measures for maternal mortality are identical to those suggested to prevent low birth weight: prenatal care, appropriate nutrition, low usage of alcohol and cigarettes, and education for both men and women about the relationship between successful pregnancy outcomes and healthful lifestyles.

Factors Affecting Birth Outcomes

Socioeconomic Status

A common explanation for high black infant mortality is the greater proportion of blacks who are poor. In fact, infant mortality rates are known to be sensitive to economic instability (Brenner, 1973). However, there is an excess of black infant mortality beyond that explained by socioeconomic status (SES). Using education as an index of socioeconomic status, table 2-5 shows a race effect over and above the SES effect. The black infant mortality rate greatly exceeds the white rate at each level of education. In fact, blacks with some college education have more infant mortality than whites with no more than an eighth-grade education.

Table 2-3

Percent of Live Births of Infants Weighing Less than 2,500 Grams at Birth,
by Race, Average Annual for Periods 1975-77, 1980-82, 1985-87

Years	All Races	White	Black
1975-77	7.2%	6.1%	12.9%
1980-82	6.8	5.7	12.5
1985-87	6.8	5.7	12.6

Source: National Center for Health Statistics. (1990). *Health, United States, 1989.* DHHS Pub. No. 90-1232. Hyattsville, MD: Public Health Service.

Table 2-4

Maternal Mortality Rates for Pregnancy, Childbirth, and the Puerperium,
by Race, Age Adjusted, for Selected Years 1950-1987
(Rate per 100,000 Live Births)

Years	All Races	White	Black
1950	73.7%	53.1%	–
1960	32.1	22.4	92.0%
1970	21.5	14.5	64.3
1980	9.4	6.8	23.9
1983	7.9	5.8	19.3
1984	7.3	4.9	20.5
1985	7.6	5.0	21.0
1986	7.0	4.7	19.3
1987	6.1	4.9	14.3

Source: National Center for Health Statistics. (1990). *Health, United States, 1989.* DHHS Pub. No. 90-1232. Hyattsville, MD: Public Health Service.

Table 2-5

Infant Mortality Rates, by Race and Mother's
Education for Singleton Infants, 1980
(Rate per 1,000 Live Births)

Mother's Education	All Races	White	Black	Ratio Black/White
Grade 8 or less	17.2	15.1	25.3	1.7
Grade 9 to 11	16.3	13.7	22.0	1.6
Grade 12	10.6	8.9	17.5	2.0
1 to 3 years of college	8.8	7.4	15.4	2.1
4 years of college or more	7.3	6.7	13.2	2.0

Source: U.S. Department of Health and Human Services. (1986). *Annual Program Review. Centers for Disease Control, Prevention of Disease, Disability and Death in Blacks and Other Minorities.* Washington, DC: U.S. Government Printing Office.

Table 2-6

Prenatal Care Utilization and Low Birth Weight for Infants, by Race, 1984

	All Races	White	Black
Percentage of babies born to mothers who received early prenatal care	76.5%	79.6%	62.2%
Percentage of babies born to mothers who received late or no prenatal care	5.6	9.6	9.7
Percentage of babies born at low birth weight	6.7	5.6	12.3

Source: Hughes, D., Johnson, K., Rosenbaum, S., Butler, E., & Simons, J. (1988). *The Health of America's Children: Maternal and Child Health Data Book.* Washington, DC: Children's Defense Fund.

Prenatal Care

Black women are significantly less likely to have adequate prenatal care than white women, and they are more than twice as likely to have babies after receiving late or no prenatal care. Consequently, black infants are more than twice as likely to be born with a low birth weight (see table 2-6).

Health care professionals have concluded that prenatal care is effective in increasing birth weight and reducing infant mortality; yet, over 20% of white women and nearly twice as great a proportion of black women get no prenatal care during the first trimester (National Center for Health Statistics, 1990). Teenagers have even lower rates of prenatal care: some 52% of all women under 18 have no care during the first trimester, and black teenagers have a slightly higher rate of no care, 56.7% (National Center for Health Statistics, 1990). A Surgeon General's Report (U.S. Department of Health, Education and Welfare, 1979) indicated that three-quarters of the risks associated with low birth weight can be evaluated in a first prenatal visit and can be reduced by competent, early medical care. In a review of research on prenatal care done over the last decade, the Institute of Medicine (1985) concluded that the overwhelming weight of the evidence is that prenatal care reduces low birth weight. More specifically, the Institute noted that prenatal care is effective in reducing the chance of low birth weight among high-risk women, whether the risk derives from medical or sociodemographic factors, or both.

There is substantial evidence that indicates that certified nurse-midwives and obstetrical nurse practitioners are particularly effective in lowering the incidence of low birth weight and increasing compliance (i.e., keeping appointments and following treatment directions) among high-risk pregnant women (Caro, Kalmuss, & Lopez, 1988). The certified nurse-midwives are trained to provide prenatal, childbirth, postpartum, and neonatal care. They consult with physicians, and they refer high-risk patients. Nurse practitioners provide prenatal care, but not childbirth and immediate postpartum services.

The success of certified nurse-midwives and nurse practitioners with high-risk women is attributed to the communications and interactions that are more comfortable or acceptable to the patients than that with the more authoritarian physicians (Caro, Kalmuss, & Lopez, 1988). These health care professionals spend more time with their patients than physicians, and this time is more likely to include counseling and education for the patients.

Although it is widely recognized that prenatal care is of value, many women do not make adequate use of prenatal care, and this deficit occurs most often among women who are most at risk. If greater use of prenatal care is to be achieved, we must understand the reasons for the current widespread inadequate use of care. A study by the Community Service Society (Caro, Kalmuss, & Lopez, 1988) in New York City found a fairly consistent profile among the women in the late or noncare categories.

Compared with those who began prenatal care in their first or second trimesters, those in the late or noncare categories were more likely to fit the following profile:

Sociodemographic factors:
Very low income
Unmarried
Teenager
Did not finish high school
Born in the United States (50 states and the District of Columbia)

Health-related factors:
Lacked health insurance
Lacked regular health care provider
No prenatal care for previous pregnancy
Pregnancy was not diagnosed until after first trimester

Other factors:
Used drugs during pregnancy
Reported several difficulties in obtaining prenatal care
Reported being preoccupied by other urgent day-to-day needs
Reported feeling demoralized and depressed
Less positive attitude toward health care in general and
prenatal care in particular

Directly, or indirectly, poverty is an important barrier to the adequate use of prenatal care. Women are less likely to seek and acquire timely prenatal care if they are poor and/or undereducated. They are also less likely to seek care if they do not have health insurance or a regular health provider–two situations closely related to low-income status. Two other problems related to income–"preoccupation with other problems" and "feeling depressed"–also limit the adequate use of prenatal care. And poor health care attitudes and experiences are also detrimental to the use of prenatal care. An expansion of the availability of Medicaid coverage and improvement of the availability of prenatal care should work to increase the proportion of adequate use of prenatal care.

Maternal and Child Health Programs

Title V of the Social Security Act authorizes a federal program that is concerned with health care for mothers and children. It provides federal support to states to enhance their ability to promote and deliver maternal and child health care and crippled children's services. First enacted in 1935, several modifications have occurred through the years. A 1963 amendment was adopted to establish special project grants for specific maternal and child health activities in low-income areas. This law provided for grants to state and local health departments for maternal and infant care projects aimed primarily at reducing mental retardation and infant mortality through prenatal, perinatal, and postpartum care, and family planning services (U.S. Department of Health and Human Services, 1981). This program includes services such as social service assessment and intervention, nutritional assessment and counseling, as well as prenatal, labor, delivery, and postpartum care. Evaluation studies (Sokol, Woolf, Rosen, & Weingarten, 1980; Peoples & Siegel, 1983) have tended to support the generally held contention that this program has been very successful. The study by Sokol, et al., compared pregnancy outcomes of women in the Cleveland MIC project with those of women with similar socioeconomic and medical-obstetric risks who received care in a hospital. Both groups delivered at the same hospital, receiving identical labor, delivery, and neonatal care. Yet, the women in the MIC project experienced 60% less perinatal mortality than non-MIC patients.

In 1981 the federal government reorganized the Maternal and Child Health (MCH) program into a block grants program. The Maternal and Child Health Block Grant program provides basic prenatal care, checkups, immunizations, and other needed health services to low-income mothers and children. However, this reorganization had the effect of reducing funds to women and children, and within two years there was a rise in adverse maternal and child outcomes noted in national data. Although the increased infant mortality rate cannot readily be attributed to the MCH budget cuts, the associations are strong, and they are consistent with studies that show the efficacy of prenatal care. The timing of these events suggests that there might be an influential relationship between these MCH budget cutbacks and adverse birth outcomes. Another program, the Special Supplemental Food Program for WIC provides nutritional supplements to low-income, at-risk pregnant women, infants, and children. This program is seen as effective in preventing premature births, fetal deaths, and other problems among pregnant women and newborn babies. For each $1.00 invested in the prenatal component of WIC, $3.00 is saved in short-term hospital costs (Children's Defense Fund, 1988). Despite this success, WIC is provided to fewer than half of those eligible and in need of its services. Similarly, Medicaid– with its Early and Periodic Screening, Diagnostic and Treatment Services for Children (EPSDT), which provides earlier prenatal care, increased birth weight, decreased neonatal and postneonatal infant mortality and morbidity–saves $3.38 for each $1.00 spent on comprehensive prenatal care (Children's Defense Fund, 1988). Yet, less than one-half of poor pregnant women and children are covered by Medicaid, a situation more exemplary of blacks than whites.

Lead Poisoning

There is increasing realization that lead poisoning may be the most serious health problem facing black Americans (see chapter 5 in this volume). Lead poisoning is a problem for young children, not for adults. However, lead does pass from the pregnant mother to the fetus, and it is well-established that high levels of maternal lead exposure during pregnancy can result in a spectrum of adverse outcomes for the fetus. In a review of several prospective studies of the effects of low-level lead exposure, Grant and Davis (1989) concluded that the "findings are consistent with and supportive of the conclusion that intrauterine lead exposure results in impaired postnatal neurobehavioral development." In one study (Bronschein, Grote, Mitchell, Succop & Dietrich, 1989) that looked at both outcomes by maternal blood level concentration ranging from 1 to 26 ug dl, lead was shown to be a significant determinant of birth weight. This study, which used 2,750 grams as the ceiling for low birth weight, found a strong relationship between the amount of maternal blood lead and low birth weight babies—even at these subclinical levels of lead in the blood (see figure 2-1). For example, one-third of all births in this sample born to women with blood lead levels ranging between 13 and 25 micrograms of lead per deciliter of blood were low birth weights compared to 19% and 21% of the babies born to women with below 7 and between 7 and 12 micrograms of lead per deciliter of blood. Employing a more severe criterion of low birth weight–less than 2,500 grams–resulted in incidence of 6.1%, 9.3%, and 12.2%, respectively, for these blood lead intervals.

These findings are significant when one considers the level of lead exposure associated with this effect. The National Health and Nutrition Examination Survey (Annest et al., 1983) reported that 500,000 women of child-bearing age in the United States have blood lead concentrations in excess of 12 ug dl. Infants born to these women are more likely to weigh less and are therefore born at higher risk for neurobehavioral delays, disorders, and deficits than would be expected at maternal blood lead concentrations less than 6 ug dl.

Elevated levels of lead are found more often in the inner cities of large urban areas–the so-called "ghettos"–inhabited principally by African-Americans. Thus, black women who are more at-risk to lead poisoning are more at-risk to passing on lead to their fetuses. Undoubtedly these factors–a greater proportion of blacks living in the inner cities and inner cities being areas of the greatest elevated lead levels–combine to put black infants at greater risk of adverse birth outcomes.

Summary and Discussion

During the period 1979 to 1981 black Americans had an overall mortality rate that was 47.4% higher than the rates for whites among persons 45 years of age or younger. Of these "excess deaths," 26.9% were caused by infant mortality. Thus, infant mortality–the death of babies before their first birthday–is a significant factor in the overall death rate among blacks (Heckler, 1985).

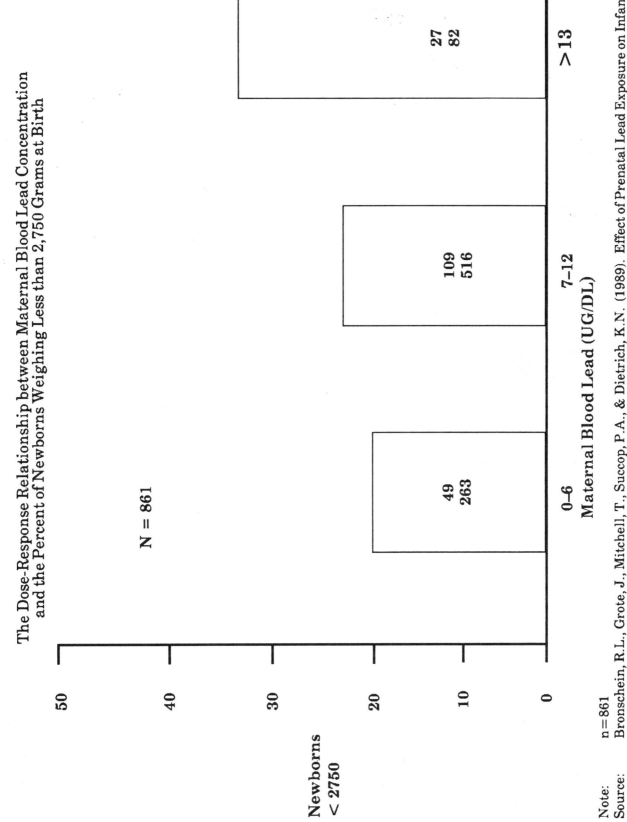

Figure 2-1

The Dose-Response Relationship between Maternal Blood Lead Concentration and the Percent of Newborns Weighing Less than 2,750 Grams at Birth

Note:
Source: Bronschein, R.L., Grote, J., Mitchell, T., Succop, P.A., & Dietrich, K.N. (1989). Effect of Prenatal Lead Exposure on Infant Size at Birth. In M.A. Smith, L.D. Grant, & A.I. Sors (Eds.), *Lead Exposure and Child Development: An International Assessment* (pp. 49-118). Hingham, MA: Kluwer Academic Publishers Group.

As we look at infant mortality, it may be helpful to remember that it is but the tip of the iceberg and is indicative of a more general problem of unhealthy infants. The two primary causes of infant mortality are low birth weight and congenital disorders, with low birth weight leading to other problems, including mental retardation, birth defects, growth and developmental problems, blindness, autism, cerebral palsy, and epilepsy (U.S. Department of Health, Education and Welfare, 1979).

Among selected industrialized countries, the United States ranked tenth in infant mortality in 1976 and nineteenth in 1985 even though the rate of infant mortality was declining in all these countries. Why does the United States lag behind 18 countries in infant mortality rates? Clearly, one major reason is the high death rate among nonwhite infants. A black baby born in Washington, DC, or Boston or Indianapolis is more likely to die before his or her first birthday than a baby born in Jamaica. Any American baby is more likely to die in the first year of life than a baby born in Singapore. The black infant mortality rate is twenty-eighth in the world, behind Cuba and Bulgaria and equal to Costa Rica and Poland (Children's Defense Fund, 1988).

It would surely seem that enlightened public policy should attempt to alleviate the great racial inequities in infant mortality, where the current rate among blacks is approximately equivalent to the white rate in the 1960s. In the United States, some 6,000 black infants die each year who would be living if the infant mortality rate observed for black infants was as low as that for white infants in the same area (Kovar, 1979). On the other hand, the white rate is already below the 1% national goal for 1990.

Generally, reformers suggest attacks on poverty-related factors. These include nutritional programs for poor pregnant mothers and infants, programs to train paramedical personnel to educate expectant mothers on the benefits of prenatal and preventive care, and, most importantly, the provision of free medical care for all poor expectant mothers and for children up to one year of age (Seham, 1973).

Before the funding was cut, Maternal and Infant Care (MIC) projects were quite successful at reaching vulnerable populations and in bringing about subsequent declines in low birth weight incidence and infant mortality (U.S. Department of Health, Education and Welfare, 1979). Although maternal and infant care providers tend to be confident that good prenatal care helps, some are pessimistic about major progress without direct efforts to eliminate economic and social problems. For example, one local program director suggested that "the most effective thing we could do is raise the employment level among young adults. That might do more than all the new hospitals and prenatal units and doctors combined" (Freivogel, 1979).

References

Annest, J. L., Pinkle, J. L., Makuz, D., Neese, J. W., Bayse, D. D., & Kovar, M. G. (1983). Chronological Trend in Blood Count Levels between 1976 and 1980. *New England Journal of Medicine, 308*, 1373-1377.

Brenner, M. H. (1973). Fetal, Infant and Maternal Mortality During Periods of Economic Instability. *International Journal of Health Services, 3*, 145-159.

Bronschein, R. L., Grote, J., Mitchell, T., Succop, P. A., & Dietrich, K. N. (1989). Effect of Prenatal Lead Exposure on Infant Size at Birth. In M. A. Smith, L. D. Grant, & I. Sors (Eds.), *Lead Exposure and Child Development: An International Assessment*, pp. 49-118. Hingham, MA: Kluwer Academic Publishers Group.

Caro, F. G., Kalmuss, K., & Lopez, I. (1988). *Barriers to Prenatal Care: An Examination of Use of Prenatal Care among Low-Income Women in New York City*. New York: Community Service Society of New York.

Children's Defense Fund. (1986). *Maternal and Child Health Data Book: The Health of America's Children*. Washington, DC: Children's Defense Fund.

Children's Defense Fund. (1988). *Maternal and Child Health Data Books: The Health of America's Children*. Washington, DC: Children's Defense Fund.

Freivogel, M. W. (1979, November 18). Infant Death Rate Stays Grim Statistic Here. *St. Louis Post-Dispatch*, Section A. 1R.

Gentry, J. T. (1979). Approaches to Reducing Infant Mortality. *Urban Health, 8*, 27-30.

Grant, L. D., & Davis, J. M. (1989). Effects of Low-Level Lead Exposure on Pediatric Neurobehavioral Development: Current Findings and Future Directions. In M. A. Smith, L. D. Grant, & A. I. Sors (Eds.), *Lead Exposure and Child Development: An International Assessment*, pp. 49-118. Hingham, MA: Kluwer Academic Publishers Group.

Heckler, M. M. (1985). *Report of the Secretary's Task Force on Black and Minority Health*. Executive Summary. Washington, DC: Department of Health and Human Services.

Hughes, D., Johnson, K., Rosenbaum, S., Butler, E., & Simons, J. (1988). *The Health of America's Children: Maternal and Child Health Data Book*. Washington, DC: Children's Defense Fund.

Institute of Medicine. (1985). *Preventing Low Birth Weight*. Washington, DC: National Academy Press.

Kovar, M. G. (1977). Mortality of Black Infants in the United States. *Phylon, 38*, 370-397.

Kramer, J. M. (1988). Infant Mortality and Risk Factors among American Indians Compared to Black and White Rates: Implications for Policy Change. In W. A. Van Horne (Ed.), *Ethnicity and Health*. Madison, WI: The University of Wisconsin System.

National Center for Health Statistics. (1990). *Health, United States, 1989*. DHHS Pub. No. 90-1232. Hyattsville, MD: Public Health Service.

Peoples, M. D., & Siegel, E. (1983). Measuring the Impact of Programs for Mothers and Infants on Prenatal Care and Low Birthweight: The Value of Refined Analysis. *Medical Care, 21*, 586-605.

Seham, M. (1973). *Blacks and American Medical Care*. Minneapolis: University of Minnesota Press.

Sokol, R. J., Woolf, R. B., Rosen, M. G., & Weingarten, K. (1980). Antepartum Care and Outcome: Impact of a Maternity and Infant Care Project. *Obstetrics and Gynecology, 56* (2), 150-156.

U.S. Department of Health, Education and Welfare. (1979). *Healthy People: The Surgeon General's Report on Health Promotion and Disease Prevention*. DHEW Pub. No. 79-55071. Washington, DC: U.S. Government Printing Office.

U.S. Department of Health and Human Services. (1981). *Better Health for Our Children: A National Strategy. The Report of the Select Panel for the Promotion of Child Health*. DHHS Pub. No. 79-55071. Washington, DC: U.S. Government Printing Office.

3

Cancer Incidence and Mortality Among African-Americans

Cancer is second only to heart disease as the most frequent cause of death in the United States. Cancer is a large group of diseases characterized by unrestricted cell proliferation and the potential for metastasis; if unchecked, it is usually fatal to the host. This disease may be contracted by any person at any age (American Cancer Society, 1986, 1987).

A disease of this magnitude is important to the general population, but the alarming discovery of increased cancer rates for blacks compared to whites suggests that the cancer experience for blacks warrants further research. Among the major racial/ethnic groups, blacks have the highest cancer incidence rate, the highest overall cancer mortality rate, and the second least favorable cancer survival rates (see table 3-1). Examining changes in incidence, mortality, and survival rates over time may provide clues to explain the differences in rates among racial and ethnic groups. These rates are interrelated. The survival rate for a particular cancer can be affected by changes in the incidence of that cancer. Changes in incidence and/or survival for a particular cancer over time can result in changes in the mortality rate for that cancer. In addition, a change in exposure to factors that predispose individuals to greater risk for a cancer will affect incidence and later mortality (Baquet & Ringen, 1986).

The purpose of this chapter is to describe the cancer experience of black populations in the United States over a 30- to 40-year time period. More specifically, trends in incidence, mortality, and survival rates will be reviewed for blacks compared to whites for major cancer (body) sites using national data. Differences between blacks and whites indicate where efforts must be directed to address the cancer needs of blacks in order to achieve improvement in incidence, mortality, and survival rates. A review of the status of the cancer problem among African-Americans will be useful in addressing strategies that may lead to eventual cancer control.

Source of Data

Descriptive patterns of cancer among blacks and whites are presented here utilizing national mortality statistics, data from several National Cancer Institute incidence surveys, the End Results Group Program, and the current Surveillance, Epidemiology, and End Results (SEER) Program of the National Cancer Institute (Dorn & Cutler, 1959; Cutler & Young, 1975; Devesa & Silverman, 1978; Mason & McKay, 1974; Axtell, Asire, & Myers, 1976; Young, Percy, & Asire, 1981). The National Offi-

Table 3-1

Average Annual Age-Adjusted Cancer Incidence and Mortality Rates and
Five-Year Survival Rates for All Sites, by Racial/Ethnic Group, 1978-1981
(Per 100,000 Population)

Racial/Ethnic Group	Cancer Incidence Rates	Cancer Mortality Rates	Five-Year Survival Rates
Whites	335.0	163.6	50[c]
Blacks	372.5	208.5	38
Hispanics	246.2[a]	— [b]	47
Japanese	247.8	104.2	51
Chinese	252.9	131.5	44
Filipinos	222.4	69.7	45
Native Hawaiians	357.9	200.5	44
Native Americans	164.2	87.4	34

[a]Data from Mexico only.
[b]Ethnicity for Hispanics was not specified.
[c]Caucasians not of Hispanic origin.
Source: Baquet, C. R., & Ringer, K. (Eds.). (1986). *Cancer Among Blacks and Other
         Minorities: Statistical Profiles*. DHHS Pub. No. (NIH) 802785. Bethesda,
         MD: National Cancer Institute.

cial Vital Statistics, the United States Health Statistics, the U.S. Bureau of Census from 1940 to 1980, and several individual studies were also data sources (National Office of Vital Statistics, 1956; Burbank & Fraumeni, 1972; Henschke, Leffall, Mason, Reinhold, Schneider, & White, 1972; Young, Devesa, & Cutler, 1975; Myers & Hankey, 1980; Reis, Pollack, & Young, 1983; Pollack & Horm, 1980; Horm, Asire, Young, Reis, & Pollack, 1984; Sondik, Young, Horm, & Reis, 1987).

The SEER Program, which is the major data source for this chapter, collects information from 11 U.S. population-based cancer registries including six states (Connecticut, Hawaii, Iowa, New Mexico, New Jersey, and Utah), four large metropolitan areas (Atlanta, Detroit, San Francisco, and Seattle), and Puerto Rico. SEER began in 1973 in order to obtain annual cancer incidence and patient survival data on specific population bases. The majority of the SEER data on blacks is obtained from Atlanta, Detroit, and San Francisco (Devesa & Silverman, 1978; Pollack & Horm, 1980; Baquet & Ringen, 1986). A major difficulty in all of these studies has been the inclusion of different geographic areas in each of the surveys and the changes in the SEER participants over time. The obvious limitation is that one cannot generalize from one geographic area to all survey areas or to the United States as a whole.

The various surveys and studies used population estimates to calculate incidence and mortality rates obtained from the U.S. Census Bureau. Rates were standardized to the 1940, 1950, 1960, and 1979 U.S. population and are presented as aged-adjusted rates per 100,000 population.

Interpretation of Cancer Statistics

In attempting to analyze trends over time, one must consider the interpretation of cancer statistics in light of changes in factors that may contribute to the increase or decrease in rates. In addition, one must consider interpretative and inferential problems that may stem from changes in data collection procedures over time, methodologic weaknesses of the health information system, and the changes in the status of African-Americans since the 1940s, i.e., surroundings, functioning, and basic life styles. The manner in which the disease is detected, i.e., changes in screening technology or practice, and the introduction of new treatment regimens also are important considerations. All of these changes and/or problems have the potential to influence the data and thereby serve as clues to the changes underway in the health care system.

Cancer is classified by the stage of development of the disease. Staging is a diagnostic process that provides a concise summary of which tissues and organs the tumor has invaded–in other words, which stage the disease has reached. Stages are usually categorized as I, II, III, or IV–in order of severity and estimate of prognosis. According to a recent report by the National Cancer Institute (Sondik, Young, Horm, & Reis, 1987), it is possible that stage definitions or diagnostic technologies may change over time to an extent that patients who might have been seen as stage I at an earlier time would be more recently classed as stage II. Assuming that treatment does not change, this change will have the tendency of increasing the survival in stage II. In interpreting survival figures by stage, it must be noted this will not change the overall survival statistics.

The Sondik et al. (1987) report further states that if detection procedures change so that a cancer is detected at an earlier point in its development, but the earlier detection causes no significant difference in treating the cancer, the data will indicate an increasing relative survival rate along with increasing incidence rate and an unchanging mortality rate.

Incidence rates will increase in the case of changes in detection techniques that lead to early detection. The tendency will be for incidence to increase by the additional persons diagnosed over that time period because of the change in diagnosis. However, if the incidence rate remains unchanged, then the increased incidence in one year will be offset by decreased incidence in later years. As a result, the cases detected earlier will not be reported in the year in which they would have otherwise been detected (Baquet & Ringen, 1986; Sondik, et al., 1987).

In analyzing mortality rates, various factors will affect the constituent numerator and denominator. Deaths–represented in the numerator–are affected by access to diagnostic facilities. Reported deaths reflect the adequacy of the diagnostic effort. The accurate completion of death certificates also is a significant factor in the accuracy of cancer mortality rate figures (Lilienfeld & Lilienfeld, 1980; Mausner & Bahn, 1974). The denominator of the mortality rate represents the population under study or the best estimate of that number. In the United States these population data are based on the U.S. census. If the census underestimates the size of the population at risk, the result is a mortality rate higher than that which actually occurs. Conversely, if the population at risk is estimated to be larger than it really is, the calculated mortality rate will be underestimated. In the black population, the former error–that of underestimating the population at risk–apparently occurs most often (Young, Devesa, & Cutler, 1975; Siegel, 1974; Boone, 1987).

Trends in Incidence Rates

Incidence data reflect the number of newly diagnosed cancer cases during a calendar year. Such data are not routinely available for large portions of the country, thus surveys of cancer incidence in selected areas of the country are the primary data sources. An obvious difficulty in these studies is the inclusion of different geographic areas in each of the surveys and the change in the SEER participants over time (Pollack & Horm, 1980).

Of particular interest is the extent to which changes in race and sex patterns in cancer incidence can be determined over time. Before looking at these patterns, however, some limitations of the data should be noted. Incidence data are not available for the total U.S. population including the black population, nor have there been any ongoing long-term incidence registries covering a large portion of the U.S. population (Devesa, Pollack, & Young, 1984). However, the National Cancer Institute (NCI) has sponsored several periodic surveys. The first was conducted during 1937-1939 in 10 large metropolitan areas covering approximately 10% of the U.S. population (Dorn & Cutler, 1959). A second survey covered the same area and was done in 1947 (Dorn & Cutler, 1959). In 1969-1971, the third national cancer survey was conducted, again covering approximately 10% of the U.S. population (Cutler & Young, 1975). Thus, during the period from 1937 to 1971, trends in cancer incidence are represented by only three points in time. The SEER program, which began collecting data in 1973, represents yet another 10% sample of the U.S. population; however, it has only four geographic areas common with the third national cancer survey. Therefore, problems in comparability result when attempts are made to analyze trends in cancer incidence covering the periods represented by the three National Cancer Surveys–1937-1939, 1947, and 1969-1971–and the two SEER surveys–1973-1976 and 1974-1984. This problem is complicated by the fact that not all of SEER registries were included from the beginning of the program in 1973 (Devesa & Silverman, 1978; Pollack & Horm, 1980; Devesa, Pollack, & Young, 1984).

Populations used in these surveys were based on data from the U.S. Census Bureau, adjusted to 1940, 1970, and 1980 figures. However, there are a number of problems with both the numerator (incidence) and denominator (population base) estimates for nonwhites (Pollack and Horm, 1980). This problem is serious enough that comparability for the two time periods 1969-1971 and 1973-1976 are questionable for nonwhites. In addition, because the original data from the first NCI survey are no longer available, analysis of trends must begin with the late 1940s. Thus, it is difficult to sufficiently assess the cancer problem in historical perspective. As a result, little information exists about the trends of cancer among blacks until about 1967. Even with the limits of this data, though, certain important trends can be discerned.

Using incidence data from national statistics for the entire United States, Devesa and Silverman (1978) observed that for the period between 1935 to 1974 cancer rates among males have increased, while the rates among females have decreased. In the past, cancer of all sites combined occurred more frequently among females; by 1974 males had higher rates than females of the same race. They also observed that during the same period white predominance in incidence and mortality was replaced by a nonwhite excess in incidence rates among males and a nonwhite excess in female mortality. Furthermore, racial differences in incidence rates among females were diminishing.

A preliminary study of cancer incidence in 1967 (Henschke et al., 1972) indicated some significant changes in cancer rates since the study in 1947 (Dorn & Cutler, 1959). The populations and geographic areas included in the two studies were somewhat different; however, the following trends were suggested. The overall incidence of cancer in men was increasing, a trend particularly marked among blacks, while in women it was decreasing. The incidence of lung cancer doubled in men and women of both races. The incidence of cancer in blacks was substantially higher than in whites–the difference was particularly large between black and white men.

The increase among men was due largely to the increase in cancers of the prostate and lung as well as a lesser increase in cancer of the colon. The decrease in women was due to a drop in cancer of the uterine cervix, stomach, and rectum. Lung cancer in women, however, increased from 6 to 12 per 100,000 population between 1947 and 1967. Markedly higher rates of cancer of the prostate and esophagus in men appeared in blacks than in whites. Among women, the outstanding differences between the races were the higher rate of cancer of the uterine cervix and the lower rate of breast cancer and cancer of the uterine corpus in black women.

More recent data on the incidence of cancers by site for men and women, black and white, are shown in tables 3-2 and 3-3. These data show that between 1973 and 1987 the incidence of cancer increased for blacks and whites, males and females. When adjusted for age, as shown in tables 3-2 and 3-3, the increased incidence was similar for each race-sex group, about 20%.

Breast cancer incidence increased among women of both races. The incidence of cancer of the uterine cervix decreased markedly among black and white women, but its incidence remained more than two times higher in black women. Cancer of the uterine corpus, which decreased among black and white women, is seen less frequently among blacks.

Cancer incidence among black females decreased in only four major sites–rectum, cervix uteri, corpus uteri, and ovary–while increasing in six sites. Among black females, the largest increases were in cancers of the lung and bronchus and the breast–two of the three sites of the largest increases among white females, who had a near doubling of skin cancers. By 1987, cancer incidence among black females significantly exceeded the incidence among white females in three sites–colon, pancreas, and cervix uteri–and had significantly lower incidence in four sites–skin, corpus uteri, ovary, and non-Hodgkin's lymphoma, a distribution that corresponds with the lower overall incidence among black females.

Cancer incidence among black males decreased significantly in only one site–the stomach. Increased incidence occurred in most other major sites, with the greatest percentage increase occurring in cancer of the oral cavity and pharynx and the urinary bladder. The greater volume of increase came in cancer of the prostrate gland in both black and white males. Black males had significantly more cancer incidence than white males in six sites and less in three sites, which again corresponds to the greater all-site incidence among black males.

The incidence rates presented have been age-adjusted to the age distribution of the U.S. population during the respective time periods covered. Age-adjusting is a statistical method that corrects for the changing age distribution of the population and allows comparisons to be made in the adjusted rates between different population subgroups and over time. As a result of age-adjusting, some of the trends we have observed in cancer incidence rates could be due to the aging of the population.

Table 3-2

Age-Adjusted Cancer Incidence for Selected Cancer Sites, by Race, for Females, 1973 and 1987
(Per 100,000 Population)

Selected Sites	Black			White		
	1973	1987	Estimated Annual Percent Change[a]	1973	1987	Estimated Annual Percent Change[a]
All sites	279.0	321.8	1.2	293.8	344.0	0.9
Colon and rectum	40.6	46.7	1.4	41.6	40.5	0.1
Colon	29.2	36.1	1.9	30.2	29.7	0.2
Rectum	11.5	10.5	0.0	11.4	10.9	-0.2
Pancreas	11.5	14.5	1.1	7.5	7.3	0.5
Lung and bronchus	20.7	37.5	5.4	17.9	38.7	5.4
Melanoma of the skin	—	—	—	5.8	10.1	3.8
Breast	67.8	90.9	2.0	83.8	115.9	1.8
Cervix uteri	29.5	15.1	-4.6	12.7	7.3	-3.6
Corpus uteri	14.8	13.0	-0.4	29.4	22.5	-2.8
Ovary	10.3	10.1	0.1	14.6	14.5	-0.2
Non-Hodgkin's lymphoma	5.4	8.0	4.3	7.5	10.9	2.7

[a]The estimated annual percent change has been calculated by fitting a linear regression model to the natural logarithm of the yearly rates from 1973 to 1987.
Source: National Center for Health Statistics. (1990). *Health, United States, 1989.* DHHS Pub. No. 90-1232. Hyattsville, MD: Public Health Service.

Table 3-3

Age-Adjusted Cancer Incidence Rates for Selected Cancer Sites, by Race, for Males, 1973 and 1987
(Per 100,000 Population)

Selected Sites	Black			White		
	1973	1987	Estimated Annual Percent Change[a]	1973	1987	Estimated Annual Percent Change[a]
All sites	437.8	520.1	1.6	363.8	441.3	1.2
Oral cavity and pharynx	16.5	25.7	3.2	17.4	16.8	-0.5
Esophagus	12.9	17.3	1.5	4.8	5.5	0.6
Stomach	25.9	19.8	-0.9	14.0	10.4	-1.8
Colon and rectum	42.4	58.5	2.0	54.2	60.5	0.9
Colon	31.3	44.7	2.3	34.7	41.6	1.4
Rectum	11.0	13.8	1.1	19.5	18.9	-0.1
Pancreas	15.7	15.2	0.0	12.7	10.3	-1.0
Lung and bronchus	104.4	118.9	2.0	72.5	82.3	0.8
Prostate gland	105.1	136.1	2.0	62.4	99.2	2.7
Urinary bladder	10.7	16.7	2.3	27.2	33.0	1.1
Non-Hodgkin's lymphoma	9.0	8.8	2.6	10.3	17.8	3.8
Leukemia	12.0	12.0	-0.4	14.4	12.5	-0.7

[a]The estimated annual percent change has been calculated by fitting a linear regression model to the natural logarithm of the yearly rates from 1973 to 1987.
Source: National Center for Health Statistics. (1990). *Health, United States, 1989*. DHHS Pub. No. 90-1232. Hyattsville, MD: Public Health Service.

The analysis of trends in cancer incidence is based on two measures of change: the total percent change and the average annual percent change (AAPC). The averaging of the rates is done because the statistical variability in the site-, race-, and sex-specific incidence rates for an individual year could introduce artifactual trends, while averaging tends to reduce the amount of statistical variation. As shown in tables 3-2 and 3-3, the incidence rates for all sites increased more rapidly for males than for females and more rapidly for blacks than for whites. The incidence rates for black males increased at the rate of 1.6% per year, from a rate of 437.8 per 100,000 population in 1973 to 520.1 in 1987; while those for white males increased at 1.2% per year, from 363.8 per 100,000 in 1973 to 441.3 in 1987. Black females had an annual rate of increase of 1.2% per year, starting at a rate of 279.0 per 100,000 population in 1973 to 321.8% in 1987. White females had the smallest annual rate of increase: 0.9 per year, with a rate of 293.8 per 100,000 population in 1973 and a rate of 344.0 in 1987. These changes in all sites combined are a result of the combinations of changes in the individual cancer site.

The incidence of lung cancer increased substantially among black and white men, but the increase in incidence–both percentage and volume–was greater among both black and white females. Between 1973 and 1987, lung cancer incidence rates among both black and white females increased at the rate of 5.4% per year.

Trends in Mortality Rates

Mortality data reflect the number of deaths from cancer that occur during a calendar year in a specified population. Rates are expressed as the number of deaths per 100,000 population and include those deaths where cancer is the reported underlying cause of death (Lilienfeld & Lilienfeld, 1980; Devesa & Silverman, 1978). The mortality data presented here are for the black and white U.S. populations from 1949 through 1984. The methodological notes in the discussion of the incidence data in the previous section regarding the computation of rates and trend analyses apply fully to this section.

A comparison of cancer deaths in the black and white U.S. populations during the period 1949 to 1967 shows that cancer deaths were increasing two times faster for the black population than for the white, and that this trend was more pronounced for the black male population (Henschke et al., 1972; Devesa & Silverman, 1978). The official vital statistics for whites and nonwhites–not just blacks–in the United States for the period 1949 to 1967 were the source of data. Consequently, there were limitations in the interpretation of data since blacks make up a substantial portion (91.3%) but not all of the nonwhites category. In addition, age adjustments were calculated for census year 1960, the middle of the study period.

The cancer mortality rate for both sexes combined in 1949 was 8% lower for blacks (137.5 deaths per 100,000 population) than for whites (149.1). By 1967, however, the cancer mortality was 18% higher in blacks than whites: 181.5 deaths per

100,000 population in blacks compared to 154 for the white population. The total number of cancer deaths in the black population increased from 15,419 to 29,715, a rise of 93% between 1949 and 1967. For whites the change was from 190,286 to 279,502, or 47%. The average annual rate of increase of the cancer mortality of blacks was 4.98% and in whites 2.45%. More specifically, the annual increase in mortality rates was 7.1% in black males and 3% in white males. Thus, the rates increased in black males 2.3 times faster than in white males. Among the females, the mortality rate increased 1.7 times faster for blacks compared with whites.

Until the early 1950s, reported U.S. cancer mortality figures for blacks were lower than those for whites among both men and women (Devesa & Silverman, 1978; Cutler & Young, 1975; Young, Devesa, & Cutler, 1975; White, Enterline, Alan, & Moore, 1981). However, over the past several decades cancer deaths among black men have risen even faster than those for white men. Rates for black women have remained steady, while rates for white women have declined (see table 3-4). As shown in table 3-4, from 1960 to 1987 the highest U.S. cancer mortality occurred among black males, followed in decreasing order by rates for white males, black females, and white females.

The age-adjusted mortality rates for all cancers combined decreased among white females by about 8% from 1950 to 1987; among black females, the overall rates have remained fairly constant. In contrast, total cancer mortality rates increased 21% among white males and 81% among black males during the same period.

The cancer mortality rates for all sites combined remained essentially stable between 1976 and 1986 for both males and females, black and white (see table 3-5). White and nonwhite males had declines of 0.2 and 0.1%, respectively; nonwhite females declined 0.4%, while white females increased 1.8%. However, both black males and females had higher cancer mortality rates than the white males and females.

Table 3-5 shows that between 1976 and 1986 age-adjusted rates for cancer mortality declined for most sites. The notable exceptions were increases in mortality rates for respiratory and thorax cancers in males and females, with the greater increase occurring among females, and the 8% increase in mortality from breast cancer among nonwhite females.

Trends in Survival

Trends in cancer mortality rates are functions of the combined trends in incidence rates and in patient survival rates. Thus, trends in patient survival are examined to provide insight into the relationship between patterns in cancer incidence and mortality.

The five-year relative survival rate is chosen as the measure of comparison. It is defined as the ratio of the observed rate to the rate expected among persons in the general population who are similar to the patient population with respect to race, sex, age, and calendar period of observation. The relative survival rate adjusts for "nor-

Table 3-4

Age-Adjusted Death Rates for Malignant Neoplasms,
by Sex and Race, for Selected Years, 1950 to 1987
(Per 100,000 Population)

Sex and Race	1950	1960	1970	1980	1987
All races, sexes	125.3	125.8	129.8	132.8	132.9
Males					
White	130.9	141.6	154.3	160.5	158.4
Black	126.1	158.5	198.0	229.9	227.9
Females					
White	119.4	109.5	107.6	107.7	109.7
Black	131.9	127.8	123.5	129.7	132.0

Source: National Center for Health Statistics. (1990). *Health, United States, 1989.* DHHS Pub. No. 90-1232. Hyattsville, MD: Public Health Service.

Table 3-5

Comparison of Recent Changes in Age-Adjusted Death Rates
for Selected Sites of Cancer, by Race and Sex, 1976 and 1986
(Per 100,000 Population)

Sites	Race	Males Year 1976	1986	Percent Increase in Rate	Females Year 1976	1986	Percent Increase in Rate
All sites	White	159.1	158.8	-0.2	108.2	110.0	1.8
	Other races	202.3	202.2	-0.1	119.3	118.8	-0.4
Lip, oral & pharynx	White	4.4	3.4	-22.7	1.5	1.3	-13.3
	Other races	7.5	7.1	-5.3	2.0	1.9	-5.0
Digestive organs	White	40.3	37.5	-6.9	26.3	23.4	-11.0
	Other races	57.3	54.2	-5.4	33.2	31.3	-5.7
Respiratory & thoracic	White	55.6	58.0	4.3	14.8	23.1	56.1
	Other races	68.2	72.8	6.7	14.3	20.7	44.8
Breast	White	9.2	0.2	-97.8	23.3	23.0	-1.3
	Other races	0.4	0.2	-50.0	20.8	22.5	8.2
Genital organs	White	14.1	14.3	1.4	14.9	12.1	-18.8
	Other races	25.0	26.0	4.0	20.7	15.6	-24.6
Urinary organs	White	8.8	7.8	-11.4	3.1	3.0	-3.2
	Other races	7.2	5.7	-20.8	3.5	3.3	-5.7

Source: U.S. Department of Health and Human Services. (1990). *Health Status of the Disadvantaged– Chartbook 1990.* DHHS Pub. No. (HRSA) HRS-P-DV90-1. Washington, DC: U.S. Government Printing Office

mal" mortality and facilitates the comparison of the survival experience of patient groups that differ with respect to demographic characteristics and calendar time (Mausner & Bahn, 1974; Lilienfeld & Lilienfeld, 1980).

Table 3-6 shows patient survival data over five time periods. Significant increases in survival occurred for blacks and whites between 1960-63 and 1974-76, 41% and 28% respectively. However, the survival trends remained steady with no increase between 1974-76 and 1979-84.

Data were examined for the periods 1974-76, 1977-80, and 1981-86, contrasting survival of black and white cancer patients by sex for fourteen forms of cancer (see tables 3-7 and 3-8). With few exceptions, survival for black patients with each form of cancer has continued to be less favorable than for white patients. For all sites over the three time periods shown in tables 3-7 and 3-8, white males were the only group to have significant improvement in survival across the time period. In each race, survival for females is better than for males. While black men exhibit slight improvement in survival across the years examined, neither white nor black females had any improvement.

The greatest differential in survival between the two races was for cancer of the oral cavity and pharynx among men and cancer of the uterine corpus among women. Among black males, the greatest improvement in survival between 1974-76 and 1981-86 occurred for patients with cancer of the urinary bladder or pancreas, although survival is very low for pancreatic cancer. Improvements also were notable for white as well as black male patients with cancer of the prostate gland and the colon. However, for both black and white male patients with cancer of the oral cavity and pharynx survival rates decreased during this period.

The five-year survival rates for black females actually declined between 1974-76 and 1981-86. For only a few sites was there improvement; and any improvement was minimal (e.g., 9% for cancer of the lung and bronchus, which still remained low at a survival rate of 13.7%).

Discussion

This review of cancer statistics over a 30- to 40-year period reveals that the cancer experience for all Americans, particularly black Americans, has become more severe. More specifically, there has been a substantial rise in cancer incidence and mortality rates over time, and survival rates have not improved significantly. African-Americans experienced the greatest increases in survival rates over time, although white Americans experienced the overall highest rates.

While it is uncertain why there are changes in patterns over time, a number of explanations are plausible. Over the past 40 years changes in the definition of cancer and improvements in the science of medicine have occurred. The effect of these changes on the statistics is difficult, if not impossible, to measure. These changes could result in either more or fewer entities being classified as cancer. Access to the

Table 3-6

Trends in Survival of Cancer, by Race; Cases Diagnosed for Selected Time Periods

Race	Relative 5-Year Survival				
	1960-63	1970-73	1974-76	1977-78	1979-84
White	39%	43%	50%	50%	50%
Black	27%	31%	38%	38%	37%

Source: American Cancer Society. (1988). *Cancer Facts and Figures–1987*. New York: Author.

Table 3-7

Five-Year Relative Cancer Survival Rates for Selected Sites,
by Race, for Males, for Selected Time Periods
(Percent of Patients)

Sites	White			Black		
	1974-76	1977-80	1981-86	1974-76	1977-80	1981-86
All sites	41.7%	44.1%	46.6%	31.1%	32.4%	32.8%
Oral cavity and pharynx	54.2	53.1	52.0	30.5	28.8	26.8
Esophagus	4.3	5.7	7.5	2.2	2.9	5.9
Stomach	12.8	13.8	14.7	15.6	15.4	17.5
Colon	49.7	51.9	57.5	43.5	46.0	45.9
Rectum	47.7	49.9	53.1	34.2	36.7	37.8
Pancreas	3.2	2.4	2.7	1.1	3.5	3.2
Lung and bronchus	10.9	11.9	11.8	10.8	9.7	9.9
Prostate gland	67.4	71.7	74.7	57.7	62.2	62.1
Urinary bladder	74.2	76.6	80.3	53.9	60.9	63.2
Non-Hodgkin's lymphoma	47.4	46.6	50.6	43.5	42.3	41.5
Leukemia	32.9	35.5	35.3	31.1	27.7	28.3

Source: National Center for Health Statistics. (1990). *Health, United States, 1989.* DHHS Pub. No. 90-1232. Hyattsville, MD: Public Health Service.

Table 3-8

Five-Year Relative Cancer Survival Rates for Selected Sites, by Race, for Females, for Selected Time Periods
(Percent of Patients)

Sites	White			Black		
	1974-76	1977-80	1981-86	1974-76	1977-80	1981-86
All sites	57.2%	56.2%	57.0%	46.5%	45.7%	44.4%
Colon	50.5	53.3	56.5	47.1	49.2	48.7
Rectum	49.5	51.4	55.6	48.2	36.9	44.9
Pancreas	2.3	2.2	3.1	3.2	6.7	3.8
Lung and bronchus	15.7	16.2	16.2	12.6	16.9	13.7
Melanoma of skin	84.3	86.3	86.6	–	–	67.5
Breast	74.7	75.0	77.5	62.6	62.9	64.3
Cervix uteri	69.1	68.2	67.3	62.9	61.9	57.1
Corpus uteri	89.0	85.6	84.0	62.2	56.0	55.0
Ovary	36.2	37.4	38.7	40.8	39.4	37.6
Non-Hodgkin's lymphoma	47.3	50.4	52.2	53.4	56.6	49.4

Source: National Center for Health Statistics. (1990). *Health, United States, 1989.* DHHS Pub. No. 90-1232. Hyattsville, MD: Public Health Service.

medical care system influences the completeness of diagnosis. Improvements in the operations of the surveys identified as data sources are indicated by the decrease in the number of cases reported solely via a death certificate as well as the number of cases reported from more than one source. Changes in the coding scheme used can also introduce artifactual shifts in trends (Devesa & Silverman, 1978; Sondik et al., 1987).

The calculation of accurate incidence and mortality rates depends on proper enumeration of the population at risk. Underenumeration of the population has been a problem in census data, although improvements in coverage have been made. The problem has been more severe for nonwhites (especially blacks) than for whites (Boone, 1987). However, use of Siegel's estimate (Siegel, 1974) to correct for the undercounting of nonwhites altered the age-adjusted rates only slightly (Young, Devesa, & Cutler, 1975), and none of the trends were significantly changed. The current population survey also has been used in order to estimate undercount rates (Bailor & Jones, 1980; Jones & Batemen, 1981; National Academy of Sciences, 1984).

In the more current data, analyses of changes in disease statistics may account for a number of additional factors: (1) new treatment advances and when they took place; (2) changes in disease detection procedures and screening practices and technology; (3) the time lag between the application of the screening technology and treatment technologies; (4) the time lag between the application of the screening technology and treatment technologies and when these technologies could impact on incidence and mortality; (5) the impediments in the path of application of new technology including the availability of the technology, economic issues such as the cost of the technology, practitioners' knowledge of the advances, and public knowledge of the advances (Sondik et al., 1987).

Obviously, all the above factors have some influence on the changing trend for cancer statistics, and each warrants a closer investigation of racial differences. However, it appears that these factors may be insufficient to explain what might represent a true increase in cancer incidence and mortality. Therefore, social and environmental factors may be important contributors (Graham & Schatz, 1979; Devesa, 1986; Dayal, Power, & Chiu, 1982). Environmental factors can cause changes in cancer incidence and mortality rates that can be readily documented. Where there is excess incidence or mortality in blacks, many cancers are related to similar risk factors including tobacco, tobacco and alcohol combined, occupation, and dietary patterns, and nutritional status. Risk factors are important because they are critical to the understanding of endogenous and exogenous conditions that may predispose a person to cancer development. Risk factors account for approximately 72% of cancer mortality and 69% of incidence (Doll & Peto, 1981).

Socioeconomic status is also an important factor in cancer incidence and survival and, therefore, mortality. Socioeconomic status is related to a variety of factors that influence cancer experience, including: nutritional status; smoking patterns; distribution, quality, and use of health resources; and health knowledge, attitudes, and practices. Lower socioeconomic status has been correlated with poorer survival rates from cancer (Linden, 1969; Lipworth, 1970); it is also related to increased cancer incidence for cancers of the lung, breast, and cervix (Devesa, 1986). When adjustments are made for stage at diagnosis in cancer patient survival studies, survival differences decrease between blacks and whites, and when adjustments for socioeconomic status are made, the disparities between the two groups are further reduced (Linden, 1969; Lipworth, 1970; Wilkinson, 1979; Dayal, Power, & Chiu, 1982).

Additional factors that may contribute to poor cancer survival in blacks include delay in detection, treatment differences, and biologic factors such as immune competence and response and histologic patterns of tumor (Page & Kuntz, 1980; Doll & Peto, 1981).

The study of trends over time in the incidence of and mortality from cancer in a defined population may provide clues to the etiology of disease as associations are identified comparing changes in environmental factors to corresponding changes in disease occurrence. This information may also be used to define the current magnitude of the cancer problem as well as to estimate future needs for cancer control programs.

Conclusions

A variety of patterns in trends have been observed over the past 30 to 40 years. Males tend to have higher rates compared to females of the same race. White predominance has been replaced by a black excess in both incidence and mortality rates among males and a black excess in female mortality. In addition, racial differences in incidence among females have been diminishing. The survival experience also reflects racial differences whereby blacks show poorer rates compared with whites.

Populations have undergone many types of changes that may affect cancer risk and make it difficult to discern true disease patterns. While the pattern of cancer distribution among U.S. population groups may vary, there remains a challenge to health care providers and researchers to provide an explanation for the differences observed among groups. In examining those differences, it becomes obvious that future studies are needed for epidemiological and statistical information regarding incidence, mortality, and survival; prominent factors that affect risk for cancer development; and available observations on knowledge, attitudes, and practices about cancer. Addressing these areas are critical to reducing cancer rates in black populations.

References

American Cancer Society. (1986). *Cancer Facts and Figures for Minority Americans*. New York: Author. Pp. 1-21.

American Cancer Society. (1987). *Cancer Facts and Figures–1987*. New York: Author.

Axtell, L. M., Asire, A. J., & Myers, M. H. (Eds.). (1976). *Cancer Patient Survival*. Report No. 5. DHEW Pub. No. (NIH) 77-992. Bethesda, MD: National Institute of Health.

Axtell, L. M., & Myers, M. H. (1978). Contrast in Survival of Black and White Cancer Patients, 1960-73. *Journal of the National Cancer Institute, 60*, 1209-1215.

Bailor, B. A., & Jones, C. D. (1980). The Evaluation of the Decennial Census. *Statistician, 29*, 223-235.

Baquet, C. R., & Ringen, K. (Eds.). (1986). *Cancer Among Blacks and Other Minorities: Statistical Profiles*. DHHS Pub. No. (NIH) 802785. Bethesda, MD: National Cancer Institute.

Boone, M. S. (1987). Inner-City Black Undercount: An Exploratory Study on the Causes of Coverage Error. *Evaluation Review, 11*, 216-241.

Burbank, F., & Fraumeni, J. F. (1972). U.S. Cancer Mortality–Nonwhite Predominance. *Journal of the National Cancer Institute, 49*, 649-659.

Cutler, S. J., & Young, J. L. (Eds.). (1975). *Third National Cancer Survey: Incidence Data*. Monograph, 41, 1-454. Bethesda, MD: National Cancer Institute.

Dayal, H. H., Power, R. N., & Chiu, C. (1982). Race and Socioeconomic Status in Survival from Breast Cancer. *Journal of Chronic Disease, 35*, 675-683.

Devesa, S. S. (1986). Cancer Mortality, Incidence and Patient Survival Among American Women. *Women and Health, 11*, 7-22.

Devesa, S. S., Pollack, E. S., & Young, J. L. (1984). Assessing the Validity of Observed Cancer Incidence Trends. *American Journal of Epidemiology, 119*, 274-289.

Devesa, S. S., & Silverman, D. T. (1978). Cancer Incidence and Mortality Trends in the United States: 1935-74. *Journal of the National Cancer Institute, 60*, 545-571.

Doll, R., & Peto, R. (1981). The Cause of Cancer: Quantitative Estimates of Avoidable Risks of Cancer in the United States Today. *Journal of the National Cancer Institute, 66*, 1191-1308.

Dorn, H. F., & Cutler, S. J. (1959). *Morbidity from Cancer in the United States: Parts I and II*. Public Health Monograph SG. (PHS No. 590). Washington, DC: U.S. Government Printing Office.

Graham, S., & Schatz, W. (1979). Epidemiology of Cancer of the Cervix in Buffalo, New York. *Journal of the National Cancer Institute, 63*, 23.

Greenwald, P., & Sondik, E. J. (Eds.). (1986). *Cancer Control Objectives for the Nation: 1985-2000. Monograph.* NIH Pub. No. 86-2880. Pp. 1-5. Bethesda, MD: National Cancer Institute.

Henschke, U. K., Leffall, L. D., Mason, C. H., Reinhold, A. W., Schneider, R. L., & White, J. E. (1972). Alarming Increase of the Cancer Mortality in the U.S. Black Population (1950-1967). *Cancer, 31,* 763-768.

Horm, J. W., Asire, A. J., Young, J. L., Reis, L. G., & Pollack, E. S. (Eds.). (1984). *Surveillance, Epidemiology, and End Results Program: Cancer Incidence and Mortality in the United States, 1973-81.* DHHS Pub. No. (NIH) 85-1837. Bethesda, MD: National Institute of Health.

Jones, C. D., & Bateman, D. V. (1981). *Evaluating the Quality of the 1980 United States Census of the Population and Housing.* Presented at the Forty-Third Session of the International Statistical Institute, Buenos Aires, Argentina.

Lilienfeld, A. M., & Lilienfeld, D. E. (1980). *Foundations of Epidemiology.* New York: Oxford University Press. Pp. 66-183.

Linden, G. (1969). The Influence of Social Class in the Survival of Cancer Patients. *American Journal of Public Health, 59,* 267-274.

Lipworth, L. (1970). Socioeconomic Factors in the Prognosis of Cancer Patients. *Journal of Chronic Disease, 23,* 105-116.

Mason, T. J., & McKay, F. W. (1974). *U.S. Cancer Mortality by County: 1950-1969.* PHS Pub. No. (NIH) 74-615. Washington, DC: U.S. Government Printing Office.

Matthews, D. E., & Farewell, A. (1985). *Using and Understanding Medical Statistics.* New York: Karger. Pp. 148-149.

Mausner, J. S., & Bahn, A. K. (1974). *Epidemiology: An Introductory Text.* Philadelphia: W. B. Saunders Company. Pp. 43-61, 126-159.

McKay, F. W., Hanson, M. R., & Miller, R. W. (1982). *Cancer Mortality in the United States: 1959-1977.* Monograph, 59. DHHS Pub. No. (NIH) 82-2435. Bethesda, MD: National Cancer Institute.

Myers, M. H., & Hankey, B. F. (1980). *Cancer Patient Survival Experience.* DHHS Pub. No. (NIH) 80-2148. Bethesda, MD: National Cancer Institute.

National Academy of Sciences. (1984). *Report of the Panel on Decennial Census Methodology, Committee on National Statistics National Research Council.* Washington, DC: National Academy Press.

National American Cancer Society. (1986). *Report of Subcommittee for Cancer in the Economically Disadvantaged.* New York: Author.

National Center for Health Statistics. (1959, 1969-71, 1975, 1976). *Vital Statistics of the United States (1959, 1969-71, 75, 76), Mortality.* PHS Pub. No. 79-1114. Washington, DC: U.S. Government Printing Office.

National Office of Vital Statistics. (1956). *Special Report. Death Rates by Age, Race, and Sex: U.S. 1900-1953, Vol. 43. Selected Causes.* Washington, DC: Department of Health, Education, and Welfare.

Page, H. S., & Asire, A. (1985). *Cancer Rates and Risks.* DHHS Pub. No. (NIH) 85-691. Bethesda, MD: National Cancer Institute.

Page, W. F., & Kuntz, A. J. (1980). Racial and Socioeconomic Factors in Cancer Survival. *Cancer, 45,* 1029-1040.

Pollack, E. S., & Horm, J. W. (1980). Trends in Cancer Incidence and Mortality in the United States, 1966-1976. *Journal of the National Cancer Institute, 64,* 1090-1103.

Reis, L. G., Pollack, E. S., & Young, J. L. (1983). Cancer Patient Survival: Surveillance, Epidemiology, and End Results Program, 1973-79. *Journal of the National Cancer Institute, 70,* 693-707.

Siegel, J. S. (1974). Estimates of Coverage of the Population by Sex, Race and Age in the 1970 Census. *Demography, 11,* 1-23.

Sondik, E., Young, J. L., Horm, J. W., & Reis, L. G. (1987). *Annual Cancer Statistics Review.* NIH Pub. No. 87-2789. Bethesda, MD: National Cancer Institute.

U.S. Bureau of the Census. (1970, 1973). *Census of U.S. Population, Vol. I, Characteristics of the Population, Part I. United States Summary.* PC (1). B. Series. Washington, DC: U.S. Government Printing Office.

U.S. Bureau of the Census. (1983). *America's Black Population: 1970-1982: A Statistical View.* Special Pub. PIO/POP 83-1. Washington, DC: U.S. Government Printing Office.

U.S. Department of Health and Human Services. (1985). *Report of the Secretary's Task Force on Black and Minority Health, Vol. 3, Cancer.* Washington, DC: U.S. Government Printing Office.

White, J. E., Enterline, J. P., Alan, Z., & Moore, R. (1981). Cancer Among Blacks in the United States–Recognizing the Problems. *Current Problems in Cancer, 9,* 1-34.

Wilkinson, G. S. (1979). Delay, Stage of Disease, and Survival from Breast Cancer. *Journal of Chronic Diseases, 32*, 365-373.

Young, J. L., Devesa, S. S., & Cutler, S. J. (1975). Incidence of Cancer in United States Blacks. *Cancer Research, 35*, 3523-3536.

Young, J. L., Percy, C. L., & Asire, A. L. (Eds.). (1981). *Surveillance, Epidemiology, and End Results Program: Incidence and Mortality Data, 1973-77*. National Cancer Institute Monograph, 57. DHHS Pub. No. (NIH) 81-2330. Washington, DC: National Cancer Institute.

Young, J. L., Reis, L. G., & Pollack, E. S. (1984). Cancer Patient Survival Among Ethnic Groups in the United States. *Journal of the National Cancer Institute, 73*, 341-352.

4

Trends in Homicide Among African-Americans

Homicide is a particularly significant phenomenon for African-Americans because it is the leading cause of death for young black men and women (see table 4-1). Blacks, who make up some 12% of the population in the country, account for 44% of all murder victims (Federal Bureau of Investigation, 1987). Thus, reducing homicide deaths among American population groups, particularly among young black males, is a growing public concern.

The term homicide refers to any killing of one person by another. In this chapter the phenomenon and the changing trends of homicide among African-Americans over the past 30 to 40 years will be examined.

Source of Data

Reports filed with the Federal Bureau of Investigation (FBI) by local police departments are a primary source of national data on homicides. Homicide information is reported in terms of the event: state and county of event; month and year of death; age, race, and sex of offenders and victims; weapon; and relationship of victim to offender. Data from the FBI can be useful in studying black homicide since 1975; however, it may not be useful for long-term studies involving race of offenders and victims before that time because local police departments' homicide reports prior to 1976 are essentially reports about the victims. Information about offenders was aggregated into monthly summary reports of the number of offenders classified by age groups. Not until 1976 did the FBI begin collecting data for an incident-based system. There is still, however, no systematic follow-up of cases after the initial report is filed. Therefore, if the offender is arrested within a short period of time, information on the victim/offender relationship is filed, but if the arrest is made some weeks after the event, this information may not be available, which is the situation one-quarter of the time.

Another source is data collected by the National Center for Health Statistics (NCHS). The NCHS data include information on deaths based on death certificates completed by local medical examiners, coroners, and physicians. Data provided on these certificates include state and county of death and specific date of death; victim's profile; weapon and location of assault; and autopsy information.

The Uniform Crime Reports (UCR), collected from the various jurisdictions by the FBI and published annually by the U.S. Department of Justice, are the most frequently used sources of arrest data available in the United States today. However,

Table 4-1

Black Male and Female Death Rates for Five Leading Causes of Death,
Selected Age Groups, 1981
(Per 100,000 Population)

Age Group	Homicide	Diseases of the Heart	Cancer	Motor Vehicles	Cerebro-Vascular Disease
Black Males					
15-24	78.2	6.7	7.0	30.8	1.5
25-34	136.9	29.3	14.1	42.2	7.2
35-44	106.1	129.3	75.8	40.0	29.2
Black Females					
15-24	16.9	4.2	4.6	7.7	1.6
25-34	23.2	13.7	17.4	8.0	6.6
35-44	16.3	56.0	73.7	7.0	21.0

Source: National Center for Health Statistics. (1985). *Health, United States, 1984.* DHHS Pub. No. (PHS) 85-1232. Public Health Service. Washington, DC: U.S. Government Printing Office.

there are a number of problems associated with using data from the UCR (Hindelang, 1974; Skogan, 1974) as well as from NCHS. Perhaps the most common problem with constructing rates by race is the undercounting of blacks in the decennial censuses. Two major difficulties with any national study data are the inclusion of different geographic areas and changes in the definition of homicide over time. With differing geographic areas included in different sets of data, there are often difficulties in making generalizations to all study areas or to the entire country. In addition it is difficult to combine or compare data from the NCHS with that from the UCR reports. The UCR data includes murder and non-negligent manslaughter, but excludes death due to negligence and legal interventions. The NCHS data includes any violent killing committed by one person against another.

Status of Homicide Among Black Americans

Homicide was the eleventh leading cause of death in the United States for all ages and races combined during 1987, accounting for more than 21,000 deaths per year, a rate of 8.6 deaths per 100,000 population (National Center for Health Statistics, 1990). The homicide rate in the United States continues to be significantly higher than that of any other industrialized nation (Curtis, 1985).

Black males and females have rates of homicide deaths far in excess of the rates of other racial/ethnic groups. Table 4-2 shows that the death rate from homicide among black men was nearly seven times the rate for white men in 1987. Black females have consistently higher homicide rates than white males and much higher homicide rates than white females. The homicide rate since 1980 for black women was three times that for white women and approximately 30% higher than the rate for white men (National Center for Health Statistics, 1990). Table 4-1 shows that homicide is the leading cause of death for black males and females between the ages of 15 and 34, and homicide rates among black males are five to six times the rates for black females (National Center for Health Statistics, 1985).

The homicide rate for black males ages 15 to 24 in 1987 was 85.6 deaths per 100,000 population compared with 11.2 for white males 15 to 24 years of age, a more than seven-fold difference. The homicide rate in 1987 for black males ages 25 to 34 years was 98.9 per 100,000 population, compared to 13.2 for white males of the same age group, some 7.8 times as great (National Center for Health Statistics, 1990).

Trends in Homicide Among Black Americans

The phenomenon of extremely high homicide rates in the nonwhite population is not new. Since 1914, when national mortality data were tabulated for the first time by cause of death and race, death rates from homicide among nonwhite males

Table 4-2

Death Rates for Homicide and Legal Intervention, by Sex and Race, 1950-1987

Sex and Race	1950	1960	1970	1980	1983	1984	1985	1986	1987
				Deaths per 100,000 population					
All ages, all races	5.4	5.2	9.1	10.8	8.6	8.4	8.3	9.0	8.6
White males	3.9	3.9	7.3	10.9	8.4	8.2	8.1	8.4	7.7
Black males	51.1	44.9	82.1	71.9	53.8	50.8	49.9	55.9	53.8
White females	1.4	1.5	2.2	3.2	2.8	2.9	2.9	2.9	2.9
Black females	11.7	11.8	15.0	13.7	11.2	11.0	10.8	11.8	12.3
				Ratio of Homicides, Blacks to Whites					
Male	13.1	11.5	9.0	6.7	6.4	6.0	6.0	6.2	6.3
Female	8.4	7.9	6.8	4.3	4.0	3.8	3.7	4.1	4.2

Source: National Center for Health Statistics. (1990). *Health, United States, 1989.* DHHS Pub. No. 90-1232. Hyattsville, MD: Public Health Service.

have exceeded those for white males by factors as great as 13 to 1. However, this ratio steadily diminished in the 1950s, 1960s, and 1970s; and the ratio held fairly steady in the 1980s as the homicide death rates from each race-sex group declined after sharp increases in the 1960s and 1970s (see table 4-2).

National data on the race of homicide victims during the period 1968 to 1987 are presented in table 4-3. The data show a consistent annual trend of proportionally decreasing nonwhite victimization until the 1980s. The racial profile of homicide victims changed during the period 1970 to 1978: in 1970, 45% of the victims were white and 54% were black, whereas in 1978, 54% of victims were white and 44% were black. Despite this trend, blacks continue to be greatly overrepresented as homicide victims.

In 1983 the FBI reported that for a black male the lifetime chance of becoming a homicide victim was 1 in 21, whereas for white males the chance was 1 in 131. Similarly, black females had a 1 in 104 lifetime chance of becoming a homicide victim, while the chance for white females was 1 in 369 (Federal Bureau of Investigation, 1984).

Another way of examining the differential impact of homicide on African-Americans is to consider its effect on life expectancy. In 1975 a white man at birth could look forward to about six more years of life than a nonwhite man. About one-fifth of that racial difference is accounted for by the higher homicide rates among nonwhite men (Farley, 1986).

Casual Factors

In his analysis of homicide trends from 1966 to 1975 Farley (1980) found that almost all of the rise in homicide mortality among nonwhites and a substantial fraction of the rise among whites resulted from the increasing use of firearms. For nonwhite women approximately 90% of the total rise in homicide came about because of the increasing frequency of firearm use. A less dramatic but similar trend is reported for nonwhite men.

Firearms are the most common means of committing homicides. National data for the years 1971 to 1983 indicate that about 60% of all homicides are committed with firearms: handguns, rifles, or shotguns. National data for the years 1977 to 1979 indicate that black homicide deaths are accomplished by firearms at a higher rate than white homicides (Baker, O'Neill, & Karpf, 1984; Federal Bureau of Investigation, 1984). Knives and other sharp instruments are the second most common weapons used in homicide, accounting for 18% of deaths. Strangulation, beatings, and falls from high places account for most of the remaining homicides. Death by strangulation causes 12% of homicides among females but only 2% among males (Federal Bureau of Investigation, 1984).

Local studies of the epidemiology of homicide in the United States that have taken a more in-depth view of homicide confirm the national experience and show that homicides frequently occur between family and friends and between acquaint-

Table 4-3

Race of Homicide Victims, 1968-1987

Year	White		Black		Other Race		Race Unknown		Total Victims	
	Frequency	%	Frequency	%	Frequency	%	Frequency	%	Frequency	%
1968	5,449	45.6	6,351	53.1	120	1.0	35	0.3	11,955	100.0
1969	5,740	44.4	6,984	54.1	158	1.2	36	0.3	12,918	100.0
1970	5,812	44.6	7,065	54.2	130	1.0	32	0.3	13,039	100.1
1971	6,840	44.6	8,238	53.8	207	1.4	37	0.2	15,322	100.0
1972	7,158	45.2	8,422	53.2	238	1.5	14	0.1	15,832	100.0
1973	8,031	46.9	8,863	51.8	212	1.2	17	0.1	17,123	100.0
1974	9,034	48.5	9,266	49.7	306	1.6	26	0.1	18,632	99.9
1975	9,463	50.8	8,831	47.4	298	1.6	50	0.3	18,642	100.0
1976	8,475	51.0	7,732	46.6	345	2.1	56	0.3	16,608	100.0
1977	9,470	52.5	8,176	45.3	358	2.0	30	0.2	18,034	100.0
1978	10,111	54.0	8,201	43.8	352	1.9	51	0.3	18,715	100.0
1985	11,163	56.1	8,276	41.6	—	—	—	—	19,893	—
1986	11,690	53.8	9,495	43.7	—	—	—	—	21,731	—
1987	11,128	52.7	9,487	45.0	—	—	—	—	21,103	—

Notes: Percentages may not sum to 100.0 due to rounding. "Other Race" includes American Indians or Alaska Natives, Asian/Pacific Islanders, and persons of Hispanic origin.

Source: FBI, Uniform Crime Reports. *Supplementary Homicide Reports, 1968-1978.* Washington, DC: U.S. Department of Justice; National Center for Health Statistics. (1990). *Health, United States, 1989.* DHHS Pub. No. 90-1232. Hyattsville, MD: Public Health Services.

ances. These studies also show that the role of alcohol and firearms appears to be important (Bullock, 1955; Wolfgang, 1958; Pokorny, 1965; Voss & Hepburn, 1968; Block & Zimring, 1973; Herjanic & Meyers, 1976; Constantino, Kuller, Perper, & Cypress, 1977; Rushforth, Ford, Hirsch, Rushforth, & Adelson, 1977; Haberman & Baden, 1978; Tardiff, Gross, & Messner, 1986; Welte & Abel, 1986).

Within the United States rates of homicide and other violent crimes are highest in large cities. Shin, Jedlicka, and Lee (1977) relate the high homicide mortality rates among blacks to higher concentrations of blacks in larger metropolitan areas, higher poverty, and higher unemployment compared with whites. The National Commission on the Causes and Prevention of Violence (1969) noted that violent crime, its offenders, and its victims are most often found in urban areas characterized by low income, physical deterioration, welfare dependency, racial and ethnic concentrations, broken homes, working mothers, low levels of education and vocational skills, high unemployment, high proportion of single males, overcrowded and substandard housing, low rates of home ownership or single-family dwellings, mixed land use, and high population density.

Most theories of homicidal behavior in black youths can be grouped into three categories: sociological, psychological, and environmental. The sociological theories focus on social structural factors such as poverty, broken homes, and limited economic opportunities. This approach proposes that these factors foster a subculture of violence filled with aggressive behaviors and high risk destructive activities (Gibbs, 1988). Other sociological studies attempt to explain high black homicide rates by focusing on the poverty of the black population as the most important factor. Some analyses do, in fact, indicate that when poverty, race, and regional cultural factors are related to black and white homicide rates, poverty emerges as the most significant correlate of homicide (Jason, Flock, & Tyler, 1983). Others have pointed out, however, that blacks commit much more homicide than Hispanics living under equal or worse poverty conditions in the United States (Silberman, 1978).

Psychological theories attribute high black homicide rates to psychological scars inflicted by racism. Particularly among low-income blacks, this psychological damage is thought to be reflected in feelings of low self-esteem, self-hatred, and rage that are conducive to violence against others (Poussaint, 1983). Black homicide rates are also attributed to the frustrations engendered in low-income blacks by life in a society that still discriminates against persons on the basis of skin color. This view suggests that, lacking means to function successfully in the larger social area, low-income blacks aggressively defend what is left of their integrity within the circle of their families, friends, and acquaintances. This may be a reason that many homicides develop out of quarrels over seemingly trivial issues (Bulhan, 1985).

The environmental theorists point to factors in the external environment–encompassing physical, historical, cultural, social, and economic factors–as producing high levels of stress and social pathology, which in turn provoke violence.

Contrary to popular misconceptions that murders are committed by "criminals," most murders are committed as a result of disputes between persons known to each other. A study of 1978 national data showed that 53% of all acquaintance homicide victims were black, and data for the period 1976 to 1984 indicate that some 60% of the murders of blacks were committed by acquaintances or family members (O'Carroll & Mercy, 1986). Among black males, acquaintance homicides are more prevalent than other types of homicide; among black females, family members are more often assailants.

Between 1976 and 1979, 63% of all homicide victims died from assaults not related to another crime. Among young males, nonfelony homicide victimization is similar between blacks and whites. In 1982, 65.4% of young black male homicide victims were killed during or after arguments or other nonfelony circumstances and only 11.2% of the homicides of young black males resulted from other criminal events; among young white males, the rates were 62.9% and 15.7%, respectively. Among young white males, however, a smaller proportion of victims were killed by acquaintances (38.6%) and a slightly larger proportion by strangers (23.8%) (Centers for Disease Control, 1986). These nonfelony killings are referred to as primary homicides. They differ substantially from secondary homicides, which take place during the commission of a felony and are typically perpetrated by strangers.

Another commonly held misconception about black homicides is that they result mostly from gang- or drug-related activities. However, prior to 1981 gang-related homicides accounted for only 1% of the nation's homicides. In Chicago gangs accounted for 5% of the total number of homicides in 1981. Drug-related homicides have varied from less than 10% in 1988 in Chicago to 80% in the same year in Washington, DC, which experienced a 65% increase in homicide that year (Bell & Jenkins, 1990).

Most homicides are committed by persons who are of the same race as their victims (U.S. Department of Health and Human Services, 1986). While there has been some increase in interracial homicide in the United States since the 1960s, the overwhelming majority of black homicides involve blacks killing blacks. A study of FBI homicide data for the years 1976 to 1979 found that the race of the killer and the victim was the same in 92% of all homicides for which the race of both could be identified (Jason, Flock, & Tyler, 1983). This distribution still obtained a decade later. In 1988, 95% of black victims were slain by black assailants, and 88% of white victims were slain by white assailants (Garwood, 1990).

Behavioral Models

Social and behavioral scientists have used several models to seek to explain differentials or trends in homicide. One such model is the deterrence model. This model argues that the certainty of punishment, especially capital punishment, minimizes homicide. Ehrlich (1975) argued that capital punishment has a negative effect upon the incentive to commit homicide. His investigation suggested that the elimination of capital punishment was related to a rise in homicide. According to Loftin (1977), one major weakness in this model is that it ignores socioeconomic and demographic factors. It also overlooks the fact that most primary homicides are neither psychotic nor premeditated acts. Wolfgang and Ferracuti (1967) estimate that no more than 5% of all homicides are planned or intentional.

The subculture of violence theory relies on cultural variables to account for differences in homicide rates, and its proponents argue that certain segments of society have adopted distinctively violent subcultural values (Wolfgang & Ferracuti, 1967). These values purportedly provide normative support for violent behavior, thereby increasing the likelihood that hostile impulses will lead to homicidal incidents. Black-white differences in homicide rates are explained in terms of differing value orientations. This model has been partially discredited by more recent research that shows that a structural poverty index, which combines several socioeconomic variables, is a more powerful predictor of homicide rates by state than either race or region (Loftin & Hill, 1974; Parker & Smith, 1979).

A weakness in the subculture of violence model is that it fails to explain variations in primary (nonfelony) homicide rates. These rates appear to be more highly associated with social structural factors, especially measures of poverty. Racial differences in socioeconomic status are striking, and several studies suggest that poverty may be a more significant factor than race with regard to primary homicides (Loftin & Hill, 1974; Smith & Parker, 1980; Riedel, 1984).

The subculture of violence theory is also criticized for its inability to explain how or why the alleged subculture emerged. Another criticism is that the theory focuses on value orientations of individuals to the neglect of conditions in American society that may foster high rates of black interpersonal violence and homicide. These conditions include widespread poverty, the lesser value that legal and social institutions in America have traditionally placed on black life, and the tendency of law enforcement agencies and others to attach less importance to violence that affects only blacks (Hawkins, 1983).

A third model used to explain differentials or trends in homicide is ecological analysis, which incorporates socioeconomic variables and looks at the correlation between these and other factors. In this model the black community is recognized as quite diverse. This diversity manifests itself not only in economic life, occupational pursuits, and network structures, but also in rates of antisocial behaviors. Ecologic models hold that homicides are the product of several variables operating at the macro and micro levels. This perspective emphasizes environmental factors for blacks, including poverty, unemployment, substandard housing, and stressful life events and conditions that may render individuals more or less vulnerable. When these factor are added to technological change–the rise in the supply of handguns–one can see at least a partial cause for the increase in black homicide.

These three models have been used in attempts to identify and describe the criminal personality or disposition among certain groups in certain geographic locations where there are disproportionate occurrences of homicide. Few studies, however, have attempted to test and develop models for understanding more recent homicide frequency.

Preventive Strategies

A relatively new orientation of public health is that it should concern itself with prevention and health promotion–in other words, on a broad basis, improving the quality of life. Violence, including homicide, affects the quality of life and is thus a health problem (Debro, 1988). In spite of increased homicide rates over the past several decades and the recognition that this problem is confronting both the criminal justice system and the health sector, there appear to be no known means of effective prevention short of drastic measures, e.g., total handgun confiscation. Currently, this measure is unacceptable to the American public. Enough is known about homicide risks, however, to suggest some useful starting points for applying public health interventions.

Primary prevention efforts need to be directed at cultural, social, technological, and legal aspects of the environment in the United States that facilitate the perpetuation of the nation's extraordinarily high homicide rates. Such preventive strategies would include: public education, professional education, community self-help, and interventions against mass media violence. Implementation of these strategies will require that health professionals join with others in an effort to eradicate factors that impair health by facilitating homicide (U.S. Dept. of Health and Human Services, 1986).

In terms of secondary prevention, early detection and case finding are the means by which future rates of morbidity may be decreased. In the case of homicide, such case finding requires identification of individuals manifesting early signs of behavioral and social problems that are logically and empirically related to increased risks for subsequent homicide (Shah & Roth, 1974). Adolescent and family violence, childhood aggression, and school truancy and dropout may be important focal points for efforts at secondary prevention of homicide. Such preventive efforts may be particularly useful in low-income, inner-city communities characterized by high rates of violence, school dropout, unemployment, and family disorganization.

The third type of prevention, tertiary prevention, is concerned with situations in which health problems are already well established. It involves efforts that are made to prevent further progress toward increased disability and death. In relation to black homicide, the problems of greatest concern are the types of interpersonal conflict and nonfatal violence that appear to have a high risk for homicide. Aggravated assaults, spousal violence, police disturbance calls, and gang violence may be important focal points for tertiary prevention.

In attempting to address strategies for preventive intervention that may deter homicide, a major concern is identifying and bringing the devastating health problem of violence to the attention of all sectors of society. This may be accomplished through community education and cooperation and collaboration of various sectors–health, criminal justice, education–and appropriate research.

Summary

The homicide trends reported in this chapter suggest a serious criminal justice and health problem for Americans, particularly African-Americans. Total age-adjusted homicide rates for the United States showed a decrease among African-Americans in the 1950s, a sharp increase between 1960 and 1970, and a slight decrease beginning in the early 1980s. In the late 1980s the black homicide rate was similar to the rate in the 1950s; however, because of population growth some 50% more blacks were homicide victims in the 1980s than in the 1950s. Among the most consistent findings in criminal homicide is that blacks and men are more likely to be victims of homicide than whites and women.

Because homicide represents the ultimate deterioration of personal interactions, its frequency in a given population may furnish an objective index of violent reactions to the cumulative stresses in the group. Moreover, problems generated by these tragic losses of life are larger than a simple summation of individual misery. Ultimately, a high rate of homicide disrupts almost every facet of society. Because homicide has such important legal, social, and medical ramifications, its study possesses an immediacy matched by comparatively few other aspects of contemporary life in the United States. The magnitude of the homicide problem suggests that specific actions must be taken by the health sector as well as the criminal justice system to reduce these rates.

References

Baker, S. P., O'Neill, B., & Karpf, R. S. (1984). *The Injury Fact Book*. Lexington: D.C. Heath.

Bell, C. C., & Jenkins, E. J. (1990). Preventing Black Homicide. In J. Dewart (Ed.), *The State of Black American 1990*. New York: National Urban League, Inc.

Block, B., & Zimring, R. E. (1973). Homicide in Chicago: 1965-1974. *Journal of Research Crime in Delinquency, 10*, 1-12.

Bulhan, H. A. (1985). *Frantz Fanon and the Psychology of Oppression*. New York: Plenum Publishers.

Bullock, H. (1955). Urban Homicide in Theory and Fact. *Journal of Criminal Law, Criminology, and Police Science, 46*.

Centers for Disease Control. (1986). *Prevention of Disease, Disability & Death in Blacks & Other Minorities*. Washington, DC: U.S. Department of Health and Human Services.

Constantino, J. P., Kuller, L. H., Perper, J. A., & Cypress, R. H. (1977). An Epidemiological Status of Homicides in Allegheny County, Pennsylvania. *American Journal of Epidemiology, 106,* 314-324.

Curtis, L. (1985). *American Violence and Public Policy*. New Haven: Yale University Press.

Debro, J. (1988). Ethnicity and Health. In W. A. Van Horne (Ed.), *Ethnicity and Health*. Madison: Board of Regents, The University of Wisconsin System.

Ehrlich, I. (1975). The Deterrent Effect of Capital Punishment: A Question of Life and Death. *American Economic Review, 65,* 397-417.

Farley, F. (1980). Homicide Trends in the United States. *Demography, 17* (2), 177-188.

Farley, R. (1986). Homicide Trends in the United States. In D. F. Hawkins (Ed.), *Homicide Among Black Americans*, pp. 13-28. Lanham, MD: University Press of America.

Federal Bureau of Investigation, Uniform Crime Reports. (1984). *Crime in the United States*. Washington, DC: U.S. Department of Justice.

Federal Bureau of Investigation, Uniform Crime Reports. (1987). *Crime in the United States: 1986*. Washington, DC: U.S. Department of Justice.

Garwood, A. N. (1990). *Black Americans: A Statistical Source Book*. Boulder, CO: Numbers and Concepts.

Gibbs, J. T. (1988). The New Morbidity: Homicide, Suicide, Accidents, and Life-Threatening Behaviors. In J. T. Gibbs (Ed.), *Young, Black and Male in America: An Endangered Species*. New York: Auburn House.

Haberman, P. W., & Baden, M. M. (1978). *Alcohol, Other Drugs and Violence*. New York: Oxford University Press.

Hawkins, D. F. (1983). Black and White Homicide Differentials: Alternatives to an Inadequate Theory. *Criminal Justice and Behavior, 10,* 407-440.

Herjanic, M., & Meyers, D. A. (1976). Notes on Epidemiology of Homicide. *Forensic Science, 8,* 235-245.

Hindelang, M. J. (1974). The Uniform Crime Reports Revisited. *Journal of Criminal Justice, 2,* 1-17.

Jason, J., Flock, M., & Tyler, C. W. (1983). A Comparison of Primary and Secondary Homicides in the United States. *American Journal of Epidemiology, 117* (3), 309-319.

Loftin, C. K. (1977). *Alternative Estimates of the Impact of Certainty and Severity of Punishment on Levels of Homicide in American States.* Presented at the Annual Meeting of the American Sociological Association, Chicago, Illinois.

Loftin, C., & Hill, R. H. (1974). Regional Subculture and Homicide: An Examination of the Gastil-Hackney Thesis. *American Sociological Review, 29,* 714-724.

National Center for Health Statistics. (1985). *Health, United States, 1985.* DHHS Pub. No. 86-1232. Public Health Service. Washington, DC: U.S. Government Printing Office.

National Center for Health Statistics. (1990). *Health, United States, 1989.* DHHS Pub. No. 90-1232. Hyattsville, MD: Public Health Service.

National Commission on the Causes and Prevention of Violence. (1969). *Crimes of Violence, Vol. 12, A Staff Report.* Washington, DC: U.S. Government Printing Office.

O'Carroll, P. W., & Mercy, J. A. (1986). Pattern and Recent Trends in Black Homicide. In D. F. Hawkins (Ed.), *Homicide Among Black Americans,* pp. 29-42. Lanham, MD: University Press of America.

Parker, R. N., & Smith, M. D. (1979). Deterrence, Poverty and Type of Homicide. *American Journal of Sociology, 85,* 614-624.

Pokorny, A. D. (1965). A Comparison of Homicides in Two Cities. *Journal of Criminal Law, Criminology and Police Science, 56,* 479-486.

Poussaint, A. F. (1983). Black on Black Homicide: A Psychological Political Perspective. *Victimology, 8,* 161-169.

Riedel, M. (1984). *Blacks and Homicide. The Criminal Justice System and Blacks.* New York: Daniel, Clark Beardman Co. Pp. 51-60.

Rushforth, N. B., Ford, A. B., Hirsch, C. S., Rushforth, N. M., & Adelson, L. (1977). Violent Death in a Metropolitan County: Changing Patterns in Homicide (1958-74). *The New England Journal of Medicine, 297,* 531-538.

Shah, S. A., & Roth, L. H. (1974). Some Considerations Pertaining to Prevention. In D. Glaser (Ed.). *Handbook of Criminality.* Chicago: Rand McNally.

Shin, Y., Jedlicka, D., & Lee, E. S. (1977). Homicide Among Blacks. *Phylon, 38,* 398-407.

Silberman, C. E. (1978). *Criminal Violence, Criminal Justice.* New York: Random House.

Skogan, W. G. (1974). The Validity of Official Crime Statistics. An Empirical Investigation. *Social Science Quarterly, 55,* 25-38.

Smith, M. D., & Parker, R. N. (1980). Type of Homicide and Variation in Regional Rates. *Social Forces, 59 ,* 146-157.

Tardiff, K., Gross, E. M., & Messner, S. F. (1986). A Study of Homicides in Manhattan, 1981. *American Journal of Public Health, 76* (2), 139-143.

U.S. Department of Health and Human Services. (1986). *Report of the Secretary's Task Force on Black and Minority Health. Vol. 5, Homicide, Suicide and Unintentional Injuries.* DHHS Pub. No. 491-313-44710. Bethesda, MD: U.S. Government Printing Office.

Voss, H. L., & Hepburn, J. R. (1968). Patterns in Criminal Homicide in Chicago. *Journal of Criminal Law, Criminology and Police Science, 59,* 499-508.

Welte, J. W., & Abel, E. L. (1986). Homicide and Race in Erie County, New York. *American Journal of Epidemiology, 124,* 666-670.

Wolfgang, M. E. (1958). *Patterns in Criminal Homicide.* Philadelphia: University of Pennsylvania Press.

Wolfgang, M. E., & Ferracuti, F. (1967). *The Subculture of Violence: Toward an Integrated Theory of Criminology.* London: Tavistock.

5

Lead Poisoning: The Invisible Epidemic

Lead, present in paint, dust, and soil, is possibly the most important toxic waste problem in the United States in terms of seriousness and extent of impact on human health. Millions of dollars have been spent to clean up hazardous waste sites involving toxic substances whose health effects are still controversial, while lead, a toxic substance with confirmed damaging and permanent health effects on extremely large numbers of children, has not been the target for aggressive cleanup action in our urban centers.

Lead poisoning is a serious but preventable childhood disease, caused by exposure to lead found primarily in paint, soil, and household dust. Children come in contact with these sources of lead during normal indoor and outdoor play. A child can be poisoned from a single high dose of lead or from small amounts of lead ingested over time. Lead can cause damage to the brain, nervous system, and kidneys, as well as affect the building of red blood cells. Even low levels of lead can result in problems with physical coordination, learning, or behavior. Most children who are lead poisoned show no signs of being sick. But even children who seem well can be experiencing harmful effects from lead in their systems. Lead is especially dangerous to children under six years of age because this is an important time in their growth and development.

Since some of the principal sources of lead in the environment are flaking paint from old houses, auto emissions, and industrial sources, old inner-city areas are the primary sites for lead poisoning. It is not surprising then that blacks experience a higher rate of lead poisoning than other ethnic/racial groups, as they are the primary inner-city dwellers. Data from the late 1970s show that black children are more than six times as likely as white children (12.2% to 2%) to have elevated levels of lead in their blood (Office of Environmental Affairs, 1985).

Sources of Lead

The most important sources of lead ingested or absorbed by children are lead paint, dust, and soil. Before the virtual elimination of lead from gasoline, airborne lead derived from the combustion of leaded gasoline provided a significant portion of lead exposure in both adults and children. This percentage has declined considerably in recent years and will continue to do so as the number of vehicles consuming leaded gasoline becomes smaller and smaller. However, airborne lead will still be an important source for children living near some industrial sources.

Soil lead derives from the deposition, or "fallout," of airborne lead and, even more importantly, from the deterioration of exterior leaded paint. The potential health effects of lead paint that has deteriorated into dust, weathered, or been scraped into soil are increased by the small particle size (which enhances absorption) and by its pervasiveness in children's environment. In particular, hand-to-mouth transfer of lead-contaminated dust and dirt during children's normal play is considered to be the primary means of the development and maintenance of subclinical chronic lead intoxication, which constitutes over 90% of all child lead poisoning (Charney, 1982).

Despite a 1977 ruling by the Consumer Product Safety Commission that limits the lead content of newly applied residential paints, millions of housing units throughout the nation still contain previously applied lead paint. Older houses that are dilapidated or that are being renovated are a particular danger to children.

House dust is a particularly important exposure because it is the final common pathway to the child from several sources. Soil lead is tracked into a house and airborne lead enters through windows and doors. Correlations have been established between the amount of lead in house dust, on children's hands, and in their blood.

Effects of Lead on the Human Body

To many, the phrase "lead poisoning" evokes the image of a child eating paint chips peeled off the walls of a deteriorated inner-city dwelling. To be sure, children living in such circumstances are at great risk of lead poisoning, and the ingestion of leaded paint is the route that yields the most concentrated exposure to this metal. Like most stereotypes, however, this one has proven to be too simple a characterization of the problem. In the past decade, dramatic advances in our understanding of the epidemiology of childhood lead exposure have led to an increasing acceptance of a syndrome of "subclinical" or "silent" lead toxicity. In other words, children with lead levels that are not high enough to produce clinical symptoms may, nevertheless, suffer serious health effects.

Young children (six months to five years) are the group at greatest risk of lead poisoning. Because of their physiology and behavior, they generally experience greater exposure than do adults living in the same environment. In terms of physiology, the blood lead levels of children rise more than the blood lead levels of adults in response to an increase in dietary or air lead levels because, on a body weight basis, they eat more and breathe a greater volume of air than adults. Furthermore, the metabolism of lead differs in children and adults. Children's absorption of lead from the gut is more efficient, especially in the presence of certain nutritional deficiencies that are common among children (e.g., iron, calcium, zinc). Also, a greater fraction of a child's total body lead burden is metabolically active rather than sequestered in bone.

In general, while lead's toxicity in adults is expressed in peripheral nervous system dysfunction (e.g., motor weaknesses), effects in children usually involve the central nervous system. The developing nervous system of growing children is especially vulnerable. Lead absorbed into the bodies of children has greater access to the brain because of the incomplete development of the cellular barrier that protects this critical organ from toxic substances in the blood. The greater cellular metabolism of the immature brain makes it vulnerable to the adverse effects of lead on cell respiration and oxygen transport. Excessive exposure may alter the number or organization of connections between neurons, or the communication between them, perhaps resulting in irreversible changes in structure and function (Special Massachusetts Legislative Commission on Lead Poisoning Prevention, n.d.).

An example of the behavior of children that puts them at risk to a greater exposure to lead than adults is that most of them engage in some hand-to-mouth activity, an age-appropriate form of exploratory behavior. This behavior may cause a child to ingest lead-bearing materials, such as household dust or yard soil, that would pose little danger to adults. A small number of children engage in pica, the pathological ingestion of nonfood items, and these children are at especially high risk because they may consume lead paint chips. A thumbnail-size paint chip that is 50% lead and weighs one gram will deliver a dose of 50,000 micrograms of toxic poisoning to a child, far above the safe daily intake.

Chronic exposure to low levels of lead in the environment is strongly associated with irreversible impairment of mental and physical health. Data on the effects and incidence of lead poisoning suggest that 25% to 50% of poor urban blacks are being critically and permanently brain-damaged as a result of passive exposure to this well-known and well-characterized toxin. Studies have shown that children suffer permanent neurodevelopmental deficits as a result of lead exposures–at times even below those exposures regarded as safe (Smith, Grant, & Sors, 1989). These deficits include a range of attention span, conceptual, organizational, impulse and frustration control, language, auditory, persistence, motor speed, visual/motor integration, I.Q., and overall functioning deficits.

Lead toxicity is mainly evident in the red blood cells, the central and peripheral nervous system, and the kidneys. Lead also has adverse effects on reproduction in both males and females, and recent data suggest that prenatal exposure to low levels of lead may be related to minor congenital abnormalities (Needleman, Rabinowitz, Leviton, Linn, & Schoenbaum, 1984). An association has been found between babies' prenatal lead exposure and their achievement of developmental milestones in the first few years of life (e.g., visual motor coordination, language acquisitions, and memory)(Bellinger, 1991).

Knowledge about what constitutes lead poisoning among children has changed over the past decade. Previously, it was often presented as encephalopathy, a disease of the brain associated with children ingesting peeling lead paint. Today lead poisoning is recognized as a largely "asymptomatic" condition, characterized by an elevated blood lead level, linked with many sources of exposure, and affecting a broader range of children.

The effects of lead toxicity are nonspecific and not readily identifiable. Any number of behavioral and biochemical changes may result. Parents, teachers, and clinicians may see altered behaviors in children, such as attention disorders, learning disabilities, or emotional disturbances, resulting from lead toxicity. Because of the large number of children susceptible to lead poisoning, these adverse effects are a major cause of concern.

Some of the symptoms of lead toxicity are fatigue, pallor, malaise, loss of appetite, irritability, sleep disturbance, sudden behavioral change, and developmental regression. More serious symptoms include clumsiness, muscular irregularities (ataxia), weakness, abdominal pain, persistent vomiting, constipation, and changes in consciousness due to early encephalopathy (disease of the brain).

The most severe effects of lead (acute encephalopathy, seizure, coma, and death) occur at blood lead levels of 80 to 100 micrograms of lead per deciliter of whole blood (ug/dl) and over. However, even moderately elevated blood lead levels (as low as 25 ug/dl) have effects on central nervous system functions. These less obvious effects occur in such central nervous system functions as intelligence, behavior control, fine motor coordination, neurological dysfunction, and motor impairment. Further metabolic effects occur in children with blood level concentrations as low as 10 to 15 ug/dl. Recent studies strongly suggest that at even subclinical (or "nonovert") levels of lead intoxication children sustain permanent cognitive and behavioral damage that manifests itself in poor school performance and a variety of learning disabilities.

In recognition of this new data, the Environmental Protection Agency has set 10 to 15 ug/dl as the threshold for neuropsychological impairment in infants and children. Significantly, 55% of poor black children exceed 15 ug/dl (Needleman, 1989).

Recent studies of nonovert lead intoxication of children have revealed a number of adverse effects. For example, one study found that seven times as many lead-exposed children were repeating grades in school or being referred to the school psychologist. High risk lead exposure groups have been found to do more poorly on I.Q. and other types of psychometric tests than referent control groups with lower lead exposures (Grant & Davis, 1989).

In studies of nonovertly lead intoxicated children lower lead body burdens (7 to 12 ug/dl, low; and 13 to 24 ug/dl, elevated) are examined by psychometric measures, particularly I.Q. tests. In a pioneering study by Needleman et al. (1979) the deciduous teeth of children were studied, and significant differences were found between the low and elevated lead groups on decrements in I.Q. scores. Other studies of children in general pediatric populations have found significant differences in I.Q. scores, developmental skills, and behavior (usually as measured by the classroom teacher) between those children with low levels and those with elevated blood lead levels. Although some of these studies have methodological weaknesses, especially the early ones conducted in the 1970s, more recent studies have improved on the methodologies and reached similar results (Smith, 1989).

In an 11-year follow-up study of subjects from the 1979 study, Needleman and his colleagues (Needleman, Schell, Bellinger, Leviton, & Alfred, 1989) found that impairment in neurobehavioral function was related to the body lead burden of children when they were six and seven years of age. The young people with higher lead levels at six or seven years of age were much more likely to drop out of high school or have a reading disability. Higher lead levels in childhood were also associated with lower class standing in high school, increased absenteeism, lower vocabulary scores, and poorer hand-eye coordination.

While attention is currently being given to the impact of lead on psychological functioning (i.e., intelligence, perception, and learning), very little data have been collected on higher order behaviors that shape a child's social adaptation (Smith, Grant, & Sors, 1989). Low-dose as well as high-dose exposure to lead has been associated with behavior subsumed under the attention deficit syndrome, which is a well-established risk factor for antisocial behavior. Thus, we have the proposition that in addition to cognitive and behavioral damage, lead exposure may also lead to antisocial behavior.

Effects of Lead on the Fetus

Many children are born with the effects of lead poisoning as a result of their mother's body lead burden. In such cases, maternal lead exposures are believed to predate the pregnancy. Researchers have uncovered adverse health effects to fetuses and infants from relatively low levels of blood lead. Gestational age, birth weight, and postnatal neurobehavioral development have been found by several prospective studies to be affected by low and elevated blood lead levels (Grant & Davis, 1989). These studies are consistent in their conclusions: intrauterine lead exposure results in impaired postnatal neurobehavioral development. They show that lead concentrations in the mother of 10 to 15 ug/dl, and possibly lower, are related to developmental deficits from early exposure.

The implications of these findings are straightforward: about 27% of all U.S. women of childbearing age had blood lead level concentrations of 10 ug/dl or more in 1980 (National Center for Health Statistics, 1981); thus, nearly one million infants may have been born in the United States in 1980 to mothers with maternal lead levels high enough to put the infants at risk of developmental impairments.

In one case, a mother's newborn was apparently poisoned through the mobilization during fetal development of bone lead stores accumulated in the mother at the time of her own preschool lead poisoning (Jones, Gutierrez, Rabin, Gonzales, & Weitzman, 1987). The implication is that two generations of one family may have suffered permanent neurological disability as a result of one exposure episode. For female infants, a third generation may be at similar risk.

Detecting and Managing Lead Levels

Since 1970 the means of detecting and managing children exposed to lead has changed substantially. Before the mid-1960s a level below 60 ug/dl was not considered dangerous enough to require intervention. By 1975, as a result of more experience with this phenomenon, the level at which intervention is suggested declined 50%, to 30 ug/dl. In that year the Center (now Centers) for Disease Control (CDC) published the study, *Increased Lead Absorption and Lead Poisoning in Young Children: A Statement by the Center for Disease Control* (1975). Since then, new evidence has indicated that lead is toxic at levels previously thought to be nontoxic. In 1990, the elevated blood level at which medical intervention is recommended was set by the Centers for Disease Control at 25 ug/dl or greater. Beginning in 1991, intervention was mandated at 15 ug/dl or greater.

Average blood levels for the U.S. population have been established by the Second National Health and Nutrition Examination Survey (NHANES II) (National Center for Health Statistics, 1981), and lead-contaminated soil and dust have emerged as important contributors to blood lead levels, as has leaded gasoline through its contribution to soil and dust lead levels. An increasing body of data supports the view that lead, even at levels previously thought to be "safe," is toxic to the developing central nervous system, and screening programs have revealed the extent of lead poisoning in target populations.

The NHANES II survey, conducted from 1976 to 1980, showed that children from all geographic areas and socioeconomic groups are at risk of lead poisoning. Data from that survey indicate that nearly 4% (3.9%) of all children in the United States under the age of five years had blood lead levels of 30 ug/dl or more.

There are, however, race and class differences in lead poisoning. Two percent of white children had elevated blood lead levels, but 12.2% of black children had elevated levels. Furthermore, among black children living in the cores of large cities and in families with annual incomes of less than $6,000, the prevalence of levels of 30 ug/dl or more was 18.6% (Annest et al., 1983; Mahaffey, Annest, Roberts, & Murphy, 1982). An estimated 8% to 11% of poor black children in inner cities have over 25 ug/dl (Pollack, 1989). In fact, the mean blood lead level of black children, ages six months to five years, living in large urban areas was 23 ug/dl, nearly matching the level regarded as elevated throughout the 1980s (Bellinger, 1989).

As described so far, the lead poisoning phenomenon would appear to be only a class issue–blacks are affected at relatively high rates because they happen to live in the areas where lead is abundant. However, lead poisoning is not strictly a class issue. For example, it has been demonstrated that some of the excess black infant mortality rate and adverse birth outcomes among blacks are independent of class: there is a race effect over and above the class effect (Reed, 1986). In very recent years we have learned that lead affects the fetuses of pregnant women and that these effects may lead to adverse birth outcomes, including infant mortality. It is highly possible that the excess adverse birth outcomes of middle-class blacks who live in poor urban neighborhoods are a result of forces that maintain the high level of residential segregation of African-Americans in this country (see Moss & Reed, 1990). In fact, the Kerner Commission Report predicted in the 1960s that blacks would have difficulty moving out of the inner cities if the current white racial attitudes continued to exist (United States Kerner Commission, 1968).

Conclusion

In a 1969 address to the Scientists Committee on Public Information, Rene Dubos observed the national problem of lead poisoning and issued the following warning: "The problem is so well defined, so neatly packaged, with both causes and cures known, that if we don't eliminate this social crime, our society deserves all the disasters that have been forecast it" (Needleman, 1989).

Recent studies strongly suggest that with even subclinical levels of lead intoxication children sustain permanent cognitive and behavioral damage that manifests itself in poor school performance and a variety of learning disabilities. It is estimated that 17% of all U.S. preschool children have blood lead levels over 15 ug/dl–the point currently used to specify elevated lead level (Pollock, 1989). The rates are higher in inner cities because of the concentration of old buildings, previous auto emissions from leaded gasoline, and industrial plants, among other sources. Consequently, black children are affected with disproportionately high rates of lead poisoning, as they are also concentrated in these urban areas.

In recent years we have been learning more and more about the harmful effects of lead. On the other hand, we have known for a long time how to treat or prevent lead poisoning. Most of the attention, however, has been focused on tertiary prevention–treating lead poisoning after it occurs–or secondary prevention–detecting elevated blood levels early on. The objective of secondary prevention is early and effective intervention to stem the progress and alleviate the effects of a disease, and this is done mostly through screening the blood of infants. At the point of secondary prevention, though, significant damage may have already occurred. Consequently, it is best to emphasize primary prevention, to remove the cause of the disease–lead–before it can do harm.

Primary prevention of lead poisoning would require federal and state agencies to consider lead as it considers other hazardous substances. The lack of commitment to an important toxic problem in our inner cities such as lead poisoning is a reflection of a relative disregard for the environmental problems of the inner city as compared to white middle-class communities.

Soil and dust found outside of residential homes is the primary source of lead that finds its way into the bodies of young children. A federal program and funds already exist for the external cleanup of lead in the form of the Superfund Programs of the Environmental Protection Agency (EPA). This is an unusual situation: we have the knowledge, a program, and the funds; yet, very little is being done. Lead is one of the toxic substances that the EPA Superfund was designed to remove, and it has begun to remove lead, but only in some suburban communities. Through 1990 not a single inner-city site had been cleaned of lead-contaminated soil, while several hundred suburban sites have been cleaned.[1]

The lead poisoning of U.S. children can be solved by integrating the issue of lead in the environment into the general program of hazardous waste and toxic disposal, i.e., with the EPA Superfund. This is not currently being done, as much of the Superfund effort is directed at removing hazardous waste and toxic substances that have less clear-cut health effects than lead. There should be a reassessment of how resources are allocated in such programs and some redirection of resources on the basis of greatest need.

Notes

1.   Reported by an EPA office at the conference sponsored by the Society for Environmental Geochemistry and Health, in Cincinnati, Ohio, July 9-12, 1990. However, three demonstration programs have been carried out in inner cities as a result of the congressional directive in the Superfund Amendments and Reauthorization Act of 1987. See Reed, W. (1988). The Lead Poisoning Epidemic. *Trotter Institute Review, 2* (2): 3-4.

References

Annest, J. L., Pinkle, J. L., Makuz, D., Neese, J. W., Bayse, D. D., & Kovar, M. G. (1983). Chronological Trend in Blood Count Levels between 1976 and 1980. *New England Journal of Medicine, 308,* 1373-1377.

Bellinger, D. (1989). Prenatal/Early Postnatal Exposure to Lead and Risk of Developmental Impairment. In N. Paul (Ed.), *Research in Infant Assessment*. March of Dimes Birth Defects Foundation, Original Article Series, 25 (6), 73-97.

Bellinger, D. (1991). Children Exposed to Lead–Clear & Present Danger. In *Medical and Health Annual*. Chicago: Encyclopedia Britannica. Pp, 286-291.

Centers for Disease Control (CDC). (1975). *Increased Lead Absorption in Young Children: A Statement by the Centers for Disease Control*. Atlanta, GA: U.S. Department of Health, Education, and Welfare.

Charney, E. (1982). Lead Poisoning in Children: The Case Against Household Lead Dust. In J. Chilson & D. O'Hara (Eds.), *Lead Absorption in Children*. Baltimore: Urban and Schwarzenberg, Inc.

Grant, L. D., & Davis, J. M. (1989). Effects of Low-Level Lead Exposure on Pediatric Neurobehavioral Development: Current Findings and Future Direction. In M. A. Smith, L. D. Grant, & A. I. Sors (Eds.), *Lead Exposure and Child Development: An International Assessment*, pp. 49-118. Hingham, MA: Kluwer Academic Publishers Group.

Jones, R. R., Gutierrez, L., Rabin, R., Gonzales, M., & Weitzman, M. (1987, October). Pathways to Primary Prevention in Lead Poisoning. Paper presented at the meeting of the American Public Health Association, New Orleans.

Lin-Fu, J. S. (1973). *Preventing Lead Poisoning in Children Today*. DHEW Pub. No. (HSM) 73-115. Rockville, MD: Maternal and Child Health Services.

Mahaffey, K. R., Annest, J., Roberts, J., & Murphy, R. S. (1982). National Estimated Blood Lead Levels: United States 1976-80: Association with Selected Demographic and Socioeconomic Factors. *New England Journal of Medicine, 307*, 573-579.

Moss, E. Y., & Reed, W. L. (1990). Stratification and Subordination: Change and Continuity. In W. L. Reed (Ed.), *Social, Political, and Economic Issues in Black America*. Vol. 4 of *Assessment of the Status of African-Americans*. Boston: William Monroe Trotter Institute, University of Massachusetts at Boston.

National Center for Health Statistics. (1981, July). *Plan and Operation of the Second National Health and Nutrition Examination Survey, 1976-80*. Vital and Health Statistics, Series 1, No. 15. DHHS Pub. No. (PHS) 81-1317. Public Health Service. Washington, DC: U.S. Government Printing Office.

Needleman, H. L. (1989). The Persistent Threat of Lead: A Singular Opportunity. *American Journal of Public Health, 79* (5), 643-645.

Needleman, H. L., Gunnoe, C., & Leviton, A. (1979). Deficits in Psychological and Classroom Performance of Children with Elevated Dentine Lead Levels. *New England Journal of Medicine, 300*, 689-695.

Needleman, H. L., Rabinowitz, M., Leviton, A., Linn, S., & Schoenbaum, S. (1984). The Relationship Between Parental Exposure to Lead and Congenital Abnormalities. *Journal of the American Medical Association, 251*, 22.

Needleman, H. L., Schell, A., Bellinger, D., Leviton, A., & Alfred, E. N. (1989). The Long-Term Effects of Exposure to Lead in Childhood. *The New England Journal of Medicine, 322* (2), 83-88.

Office of Environmental Affairs. (1985). *Boston Child Lead Poisoning: Request for Immediate Clean-up of Lead-Contaminated Soil in Emergency Areas*. Boston: Department of Health and Hospitals.

Pollack, S. (1989, October). Solving the Lead Dilemma. *Technology Review*, 22-30.

Reed, W. L. (1986). Suffer the Children: Some of the Effects of Racism on the Health of Black Infants. In P. Connor & R. Kerr (Eds.), *Critical Perspectives in the Sociology of Health and Illness* (2nd ed.). New York: St. Martin's Press.

Smith, M. A., Grant, L. D., & Sors, A. J. (Eds.). (1989). *Lead Exposure and Child Development: An International Assessment.* Hingham, MA: Kluwer Academic Publishers Group.

Smith, M. A. (1989). The Effects of Low-Level Lead Exposure on Children. In M. A. Smith, L. D. Grant, & A. I. Sors (Eds.), *Lead Exposure and Child Development: An International Assessment* (pp. 3-48). Hingham, MA: Kluwer Academic Publishers Group.

Special Massachusetts Legislative Commission on Lead Poisoning Prevention. (n.d.). *The Continuing Toll: Lead Poisoning Prevention in the Commonwealth: Current Efforts and Future Strategies.* Boston: Author.

United States Kerner Commission. (1968). *Report of the National Advisory Commission on Civil Disorders.* New York: Bantam Books.

6

Current Plagues: Chemical Dependency and AIDS

Several of our current national health problems may be seen as plagues. The health problems addressed in this chapter afflict a wide range of individuals and are destructive to modern society in a manner that is somewhat similar to the plagues recorded in ancient history. The so-called current plagues discussed in this chapter are smoking, alcohol and drug misuse, and AIDS.

Smoking and Health

Cigarette smoking, the single most preventable cause of death in our society, continues to decline although it is still responsible for approximately 390,000 deaths each year in the United States. In 1974, 37.1% of the population 25 years of age and over were smokers; in 1987, the proportion had dropped to 29.1%. The highest proportion of smokers was among black males; about two of every five (40.3%) black men smoked in 1987 (U.S. Department of Health and Human Services, 1990).

Smoking Prevalence

Nationally, cigarette smoking is more prevalent among blacks than among whites. Virtually all of this difference is due to the high smoking rate of black males rather than black females. Table 6-1 demonstrates these differences and compares, for both males and females, white and black smoking prevalence rates in selected years from 1965 to 1987. Although prevalence rates declined during this period for all four comparison groups, there remained a gap between black and white prevalence rates in 1987, nearly all of which can be attributed to black males. Black males' smoking prevalence (40.3%) exceeded that of white males (30.7%) by nearly a third. Black female prevalence, on the other hand, was only 0.6 percentage points greater than that of white females.

Former Smoker Status

Whites are considerably more likely than blacks to be former smokers (see table 6-1). Among males, sharp increases in the percentage of former smokers in the population occurred between 1965 and 1976, with a considerable slowing of this increase

Table 6-1

Percent of Persons 20 Years of Age[a] and Over Who Smoked Cigarettes,
by Sex and Race, Selected Years, 1965-1987

Race and Sex	Current Smoker[b]					Former Smoker				
	1965	1976	1980[c]	1985	1987	1965	1976	1980[c]	1985	1987
White males	51.3%	41.0%	37.1%	31.8%	30.7%	21.2%	30.7%	31.9%	34.7%	32.6%
Black males	59.6	50.1	44.9	40.7	40.3	12.6	20.2	20.6	24.4	22.2
White females	34.5	32.4	30.0	28.3	27.3	8.5	14.6	16.3	19.7	18.9
Black females	32.7	34.7	30.6	31.7	27.9	5.9	10.2	11.8	13.4	13.2

[a]Age-adjusted.
[b]A current smoker is a person who has smoked at least 100 cigarettes and who now smokes; includes occasional smokers.
[c]Based on data for the last 6 months of 1980.

Note: Excludes unknown smoking status.

Source: U.S. Department of Health and Human Services. (1990). *Health Status of the Disadvantaged—Chartbook 1990.* DHHS Pub. No. (HRSA) HRS-P-DV 90-1. Washington, DC: U.S. Government Printing Office.

in the ensuing nine years. White males were more likely than black males to be former smokers in each of the data collection years, with the gap between the two groups increasing slightly at each of the earlier data collection years until 1980 (i.e., 8.6%, 10.5%, and 11.3%, respectively) and lessening to 10.4% and 10.3% in 1980 and 1985. Among females, a similar pattern is observed, although the percentage of former female smokers at all points is approximately only one-half that of males.

Cigarettes Smoked Per Day

Although smoking prevalence rates among blacks are greater than those of whites, heavy smoking (25 or more cigarettes per day) is considerably less prevalent among blacks. Among males, whites are more than three times as likely to be heavy smokers than blacks (see table 6-2). The percentage of white males who smoke heavily increased approximately 41% between 1965 and 1985, from 26.0% to 36.6%. Among black males the increase in the number of heavy smokers was less than one-fourth, from 8.6% to 10.7%

The percentage of white female smokers who smoke heavily increased dramatically during this period. In 1965 13.3% of white females smoked 25 or more cigarettes a day, whereas in 1985 22.7% smoked that many cigarettes, for an increase of approximately 71%. Among black females, 4.6% smoked heavily in 1965 while 6.6% did so in 1985, for an increase of approximately 41%. In a pattern almost identical to that of males, then, white females are more than three times as likely to be heavy smokers as black females.

Opportunities for Smoking Prevention and Cessation

The evidence indicates that black Americans are more likely to be smokers and are more likely to be at higher risk for the development of many smoking-related cancers. Yet, this body of knowledge also suggests the existence of special opportunities to ameliorate smoking-related cancer risk among the black population.

First, although the overall smoking prevalence rates among blacks are higher, a considerably smaller percentage of blacks are heavy smokers. This is a particularly important point because there is strong evidence that cigarette smoking is more easily modified among lighter smokers.

Second, although blacks have quit smoking in smaller numbers than whites, the 1980 American Cancer Society survey found that more blacks than whites were interested in stopping smoking, suggesting that there may be a significant number of black smokers who, given the right resources, might be amenable to renewed smoking cessation efforts, (EVAXX, 1983).

Table 6-2

Cigarettes Smoked per Day by Persons 20 Years of Age[a] and Over,
by Sex and Race, Selected Years, 1965-1985

Race and Sex	Less than 15				25 or more			
	1965	1976	1980[b]	1985	1965	1976	1980[b]	1985
	Percent of current smokers[c]							
White males	27.7%	22.3%	20.0%	21.7%	26.0%	33.3%	37.3%	36.6%
Black males	49.8	43.7	48.4	52.9	8.6	10.8	13.8	10.7
White females	43.7	34.3	30.7	32.8	13.3	20.9	25.2	22.7
Black females	70.3	64.5	61.1	61.2	4.6	5.6	8.6	6.6

[a] Age-adjusted.
[b] Based on data for the last 6 months of 1980.
[c] A current smoker is a person who has smoked at least 100 cigarettes and who now smokes; includes occasional smokers.

Note: Excludes unknown smoking status.

Source: U.S. Department of Health and Human Services. (1990). *Health Status of the Disadvantaged–Chartbook 1990*. DHHS Pub. No. (HRSA) HRS-P-DV 90-1. Washington, DC: U.S. Government Printing Office.

The evidence also indicates that smoking is a function of socioeconomic status. In table 6-3, for instance, while each sex and race group shows a declining trend in smoking between the years 1974 and 1987, this decline is affected by socioeconomic status: the decline was greater among more educated individuals. In other words, the greater the education the greater the decline in the proportion of current smokers.

Alcohol and Drug Misuse

Alcohol and drugs are factors in a number of health and social problems. They often play a role in deaths due to accidents, homicides, and suicides, as well as from diseases such as cirrhosis and cancer. According to the National Center for Health Statistics, some 53.4% of persons 12 years of age and over reported alcohol use during the preceding month in 1988. The percentage of whites reporting usage was 55.1%; blacks, 44.3%; and Hispanics, 49.2%. For each race or ethnicity, use is most prevalent among the 18 to 25 and 26 to 34 age groups. However, among adolescents aged 12 to 17, 26.8% of the males and 23.5% of the females reported use in the preceding month (National Center for Health Statistics, 1990).

By examining the figures in table 6-4, we can gain a sense of the total years of potential life that are lost to alcohol-related causes of mortality in our society in a single year. Two points are quite clear from the data. One is that the effect of alcohol abuse is not trivial; the other is that blacks experience substantially higher rates of years of potential life lost than whites.

Except among youths, blacks are overrepresented on most indirect measures of alcohol problems. Blacks are at high risk for morbidity and mortality for acute and chronic alcohol-related diseases such as alcohol, fatty liver, hepatitis, liver cirrhosis, and esophageal cancer (Herd, 1986). Yet in surveys of alcohol use and abuse, black men and women are more likely to classify themselves as abstainers than white men and women. Also, white men report a much higher rate of heavy drinking than black men (21% to 14%) while white women report lower rates of heavy consumption than black women, though the percentages are much smaller (4% to 7%) (U.S. Department of Health and Human Services, 1986).

Herd reports that this apparent contradiction between lower use of alcohol by blacks overall yet higher rates of alcohol-related problems is probably the result of a major difference in drinking patterns. Among white males heavy and problematic drinking is concentrated in the younger ages, 15 to 25; while black males begin to report high rates of heavy drinking and social problems after age 30. This pattern of later onset might lead to prolonged heavy consumption, putting black males at greater risk for chronic diseases.

Efforts to reduce and prevent alcohol problems include attempts to lower the rates of consumption through price controls, taxation, restriction in the number of alcohol outlets and hours of sale, and raising the legal age of alcohol consumption

Table 6-3

Age-Adjusted Prevalence of Current Cigarette Smoking by Persons 25 Years of Age and Over, by Sex, Race, and Education, Selected Years 1974-1987

Sex, Race, and Education	1974	1979	1983	1987
	Percent of persons			
All persons[a]	37.1%	33.3%	31.7%	29.1%
Less than 12 years	43.8	41.1	40.8	40.6
12 years	36.4	33.7	33.6	31.8
13-15 years	35.8	33.2	30.3	27.2
16 or more years	27.5	22.8	20.7	16.7
All males[a]	43.0	37.6	35.1	31.5
Less than 12 years	52.4	48.1	47.2	45.7
12 years	42.6	39.1	37.4	35.2
13-15 years	41.6	36.5	33.0	28.4
16 or more years	28.6	23.1	21.8	17.3
White males[a]	41.9	36.9	34.5	30.6
Less than 12 years	51.6	48.0	47.9	45.3
12 years	42.2	38.6	37.1	34.6
13-15 years	41.4	36.4	32.6	28.0
16 or more years	28.1	22.8	21.1	17.4
Black males[a]	53.8	44.9	42.8	41.9
Less than 12 years	58.3	50.1	46.0	49.4
12 years	51.2[b]	48.4	47.2	43.6
13-15 years	45.7[b]	39.3	44.7	32.4
16 or more years	41.8[b]	37.9[b]	31.3[b]	20.9
All females[a]	32.2	29.6	28.8	26.9
Less than 12 years	36.8	35.0	35.3	36.1
12 years	32.5	29.9	30.9	29.2
13-15 years	30.2	30.0	27.5	26.0
16 or more years	26.1	22.5	19.2	16.1
White females[a]	31.9	29.8	28.8	27.0
Less than 12 years	37.0	36.1	35.5	37.0
12 years	32.1	29.9	30.9	29.4
13-15 years	30.5	30.6	28.0	26.2
16 or more years	25.8	21.9	18.9	16.4
Black females[a]	35.9	30.6	31.8	28.6
Less than 12 years	36.4	31.9	36.9	35.0
12 years	41.9	33.0	35.2	28.1
13-15 years	33.2	28.8[b]	26.5	27.2
16 or more years	35.2[b]	43.4[b]	38.7[b]	19.5

[a]Includes unknown education.

[b]For age groups where percent smoking was 0 or 100 the age adjustment procedure was modified to substitute the percent from the next lower education group. These age-adjusted percents should be considered unreliable because of small sample size.

Source: National Center for Health Statistics. (1990). *Health, United States, 1989*. DHHS Pub. No. 90-1232. Hyattsville, MD: Public Health Service.

Table 6-4

Years of Potential Life Lost (YPLL) and YPLL Rates per 100,000 Population for
Alcohol-Related Causes of Mortality, by Race and Sex, 1980

Cause	Race	Total YPLL[a]		YPLL Rates per 100,000[b]	
		Male	Female	Male	Female
Alcohol abuse	White	61,340	16,676	72.9	19.7
	Black	15,112	4,039	131.5	32.2
Alcohol dependence	White	98,590	27,720	117.2	32.8
	Black	52,765	19,951	459.1	158.8
Alcohol cirrhosis	White	82,921	33,365	98.6	39.5
	Black	29,115	15,141	253.3	120.5
Other cirrhosis	White	149,515	69,726	177.7	82.5
	Black	54,006	31,005	469.9	246.8

[a]Because more than one condition may appear as a contributing cause for any one
  death, data is not additive across conditions.
[b]Based on population aged 1 year to 64 years.

Source: U.S. Department of Health and Human Services. (1987). *Prevention of
          Disease, Disability and Death in Blacks and Other Minorities: Annual
          Program Review, 1986*. Washington, DC: Author.

(Herd, 1986), as well as through school and community education. The difficulty of tackling the issue through regulation and control of the industry might be why we see more action in the realm of school and community education.

The good news is that alcohol consumption rates are slowly declining. This overall decline in alcohol use correlates with lowered cirrhosis mortality rates and reductions in alcohol-related motor vehicle accidents. Overall, the death rate for cirrhosis dropped by about one-fifth between 1978 and 1987, from 13.5 to 10.8 per 100,000 population. Further, among high school seniors the general trend of alcohol use declined in the 1980s. About 6.9% of the high school senior class of 1979 reported drinking alcohol daily, while in the class of 1988 about 4.2% reported drinking alcohol daily--a 39% decrease in nine years (National Center for Health Statistics, 1990).

Use of illicit drugs continues to be a major public health problem, although marijuana use has decreased. The percent of young adults 18 to 25 years of age reporting frequent use of marijuana dropped from 19% in 1977 to 7% in 1988. Among 12- to 17-year-olds, frequent use dropped from 9% in 1977 to 2% in 1988 (National Center for Health Statistics, 1990).

Results of a national survey on drug use among the high school senior class of 1988 show a significant decrease in cocaine use for the second year in a row. In 1987 about 4.3% and in 1988 about 3.4% reported using cocaine in the past thirty days, compared with about 6.7% in 1985 and 6.2% in 1986. However, these data were collected before the recent crack cocaine phenomenon (National Center for Health Statistics, 1990).

Blacks are seen as being disproportionately involved in drugs. A common image of black urban communities is that they are places of high crime and illegal drug activity. Daily media reports propogate--if not create--this image because most of the individuals covered in these activities in the news media are black. Data shown in tables 6-5 and 6-6 indicate quite clearly that there is a significant difference between the actual criminal activity of blacks--especially drug use--and public perception.

For instance, we see that black males do not differ very much from white males in overall illicit drug use; nor do black females differ much from white females (see table 6-5). Whites, in fact, have a higher rate of illegal drug use than blacks until the age of 35. After the age of 35 black rates exceed white rates. The same comparisons obtain in the use of cocaine specifically. And, as table 6-6 exhibits, white high school students use drugs at higher rates than do black students. Only with heroin use does black student use exceed the reported use by white students.

These illegal drug use data contrast sharply with both the image consistently put forth by media reports and with the apparent activity of law enforcement officials, each of which appears to focus on blacks and the black community. Since whites use illegal drugs at least as much as blacks, and since there are some seven times more whites than blacks in the country, an equitable distribution of images of drug users in the media would dictate up to seven times more whites than blacks.

Table 6-5

Percentage of Illicit Drug Use, by Age, Sex, and Race, 1985

Age/Sex	Any Illicit Drug Use, Ever		Cocaine Use, Ever	
	White	Black	White	Black
Total	37.8%	37.2%	12.4%	9.9%
Male	42.4	44.5	16.0	14.8
Female	33.6	31.0	9.0	5.7
12-17 years	30.7	24.4	5.1	2.9
Male	31.2	28.7	6.2	4.5
Female	30.3	20.1	4.0	1.2
18-25 years	69.1	55.1	28.3	13.4
Male	68.6	62.1	31.8	16.3
Female	69.5	49.0	24.8	11.0
26-34 years	65.9	56.3	27.0	17.2
Male	73.8	61.4	33.3	23.5
Female	58.2	52.0	20.9	11.7
35 + years	20.3	25.2	4.0	7.6
Male	24.9	34.5	6.8	14.1
Female	16.4	17.9	1.6	2.4

Source: National Institute of Drug Abuse. (1986). *1985 National Household Survey on Drug Abuse: Population Estimates.* Washington, DC: Author.

Table 6-6

Lifetime, Annual, and 30-Day Prevalence of Drug
Use, by Race, for High School Senior Class of 1988

	Race	
	White	Black
Approximate Weighted N:	11,900	2,000
Marijuana/Hashish		
Lifetime	49.9%	36.6%
Annual	36.2	19.7
30-day	19.9	9.8
Inhalants		
Lifetime	18.5	8.4
Annual	7.5	2.9
30-day	2.9	1.8
Cocaine		
Lifetime	12.8	6.4
Annual	8.4	3.7
30-day	3.7	1.4
Crack		
Lifetime	4.8	3.4
Annual	3.1	2.6
30-day	1.5	1.3
Other cocaine		
Lifetime	12.8	5.2
Annual	7.8	2.1
30-day	3.2	1.5
Heroin		
Lifetime	1.1	1.4
Annual	0.4	0.8
30-day	0.2	0.5
Alcohol		
Lifetime	94.2	84.4
Annual	89.0	69.9
30-day	69.5	40.9
Cigarettes		
Lifetime	68.9	54.3
30-day	32.3	12.8

Source: National Institute of Drug Abuse. (1989). *Drug Abuse Among Racial/Ethnic Minorities*. Washington, DC: Author.

AIDS

Acquired immune deficiency syndrome (AIDS) is increasingly becoming a disease of poor, African-American heterosexuals and their children who are residents of the inner-city. In general, homosexual/bisexual males remain the population at greatest risk, accounting for approximately two-thirds of the cumulative national cases. Among black males, 35.4% report exposure to the disease through homosexual/bisexual risk behaviors and 39.4% through intravenous (IV) drug use (see table 6-7).

Precise figures of the incidence and prevalence of AIDS cases are poorly known and difficult to ascertain. It is also likely that they underestimate the true scope of the disease. However, data from the Centers for Disease Control show a total number of 104,497 reported AIDS cases in the United States as of 1989. The occurrence of these cases is disproportionately overrepresented in the black population. For example, although blacks compose only 12% of the U.S. population, they account for 27% of known AIDS cases (table 6-7).

Among all risk groups, blacks are more likely than whites to get AIDS and, after diagnosis, have a shorter mean survival time than whites–8 months and 18 to 24 months, respectively. Among all males in the United States with AIDS, 25% are black; among all women with the disease, 55% are black; among children with AIDS, 55% are black; and among IV drug users, the population where the virus is spreading fastest, 54% of those afflicted with AIDS are black (National Center for Health Statistics, 1990).

Intravenous drug use accounts for a large proportion of all new cases of AIDS, and it is not only drug users themselves who are at high risk, but their sex partners as well. Female sex partners, both drug users and nondrug users, can, as a result of perinatal transmission, infect a fetus in the womb or a newborn at birth. Forty percent of all AIDS cases among children under 13 years of age and 50% of the AIDS deaths in this age group are among infants–children less than one year of age (National Center for Health Statistics, 1990). Most of these cases of infant AIDS are assumed to be the result of perinatal transmission from mothers, most of whom are either IV drug users or who are the sex partners of IV drug users (U.S. Department of Health and Human Services, 1990).

A breakdown by race and age of deaths from AIDS (see table 6-8) reflects the distribution of cases. In 1988 blacks constituted nearly 30% of all AIDS deaths: 26.5% among males over 13, 57% among females over 13, and 52.2% of all children (under 13 years of age). It is an alarming fact that AIDS has become such a prominent determinant of infant and child mortality. It is projected that, if current trends continue, in the early 1990s AIDS will be among the five leading causes of death in children.

Very little is known about the racial distribution of knowledge, beliefs, and responses to AIDS. However, it is clear that black communities have a disproportionate share of conditions and situations conducive to the spread of AIDS. One such con-

Table 6-7

Acquired Immunodeficiency Syndrome (AIDS) Cases, by Race/Ethnicity, Sex, and Transmission Category for Persons 13 Years of Age and Over, 1983-1989

Race/Ethnicity, Sex, and Transmission Category	All Years[a,b]	1983	1984	1985	1986	1987	1988	1989[b]	All Years[a,b]	1984	1988	1989[b]
	Number, by Year of Report								Percent Distribution			
Total[c]	104,497	2,032	4,395	8,076	12,981	20,821	30,377	24,995	100.0	100.0	100.0	100.0
Male homosexual/bisexual	64,726	1,263	2,867	5,426	8,521	13,546	17,911	14,670	61.9	65.2	59.0	58.7
Intravenous drug use	20,590	367	776	1,393	2,231	3,522	6,819	5,341	19.7	17.7	22.4	21.4
Male homosexual/bisexual and intravenous drug use	7,250	200	408	595	988	1,524	1,946	1,519	6.9	9.3	6.4	6.1
Hemophilia/coagulation disorder	1,002	11	36	75	123	214	298	238	1.0	0.8	1.0	1.0
Born in Caribbean/African countries	1,530	85	110	141	220	266	375	285	1.5	2.5	1.2	1.1
Heterosexual	3,310	23	57	137	334	605	1,122	1,025	3.2	1.3	3.7	4.1
Sexual contact with intravenous drug user	2,367	16	42	101	231	419	817	734	2.3	1.0	2.7	2.9
Transfusion	2,571	26	52	168	305	630	835	550	2.5	1.2	2.8	2.2
Undetermined[e]	3,518	57	89	141	259	514	1,070	1,367	3.4	2.0	3.5	5.5
Race/ethnicity												
White, not Hispanic	61,130	1,172	2,690	4,949	7,817	12,896	17,120	14,028	100.0	100.0	100.0	100.0
Male homosexual/bisexual	47,064	927	2,160	4,047	6,219	10,045	12,903	10,393	77.0	80.3	75.4	74.1
Intravenous drug use	4,473	72	147	251	405	815	1,483	1,265	7.3	5.5	8.7	9.0
Male homosexual/bisexual and intravenous drug use	4,481	124	265	378	651	976	1,132	924	7.3	9.9	6.6	6.6
Hemophilia/coagulation disorder	848	10	26	64	113	184	245	199	1.4	1.0	1.4	1.4
Born in Caribbean/African countries	3	–	1	–	1	–	1	–	0.0	0.0	0.0	–
Heterosexual[d]	1,006	2	16	32	94	196	354	311	1.6	0.6	2.1	2.2
Sexual contact with intravenous drug user	559	–	9	16	45	101	202	185	0.9	0.3	1.2	1.3
Transfusion	1,918	21	39	130	236	475	606	407	3.1	1.4	3.5	2.9
Undetermined[e]	1,337	16	36	47	98	205	396	529	2.2	1.3	2.3	3.8

Transmission category	Number								Percent distribution			
Black, not Hispanic	28,693	546	1,088	2,002	3,288	5,228	8,814	7,484	100.0	100.0	100.0	100.0
Male homosexual/bisexual	10,626	195	402	795	1,322	2,103	3,060	2,652	37.0	36.9	34.7	35.4
Intravenous drug use	11,111	182	405	749	1,201	1,872	3,685	2,952	38.7	37.2	41.8	39.4
Male homosexual/bisexual and intravenous drug use	1,946	44	95	145	236	387	577	440	6.8	8.7	6.5	5.9
Hemophilia/coagulation disorder	65	—	5	4	4	12	26	14	0.2	0.5	0.3	0.2
Born in Caribbean/African countries	1,510	85	109	141	218	263	369	278	5.3	10.0	4.2	3.7
Heterosexual[d]	1,674	10	23	79	160	306	549	543	5.8	2.1	6.2	7.3
Sexual contact with intravenous drug user	1,289	6	17	62	117	238	434	411	4.5	1.6	4.9	5.5
Transfusion	409	2	10	26	44	93	148	86	1.4	0.9	1.7	1.1
Undetermined[e]	1,352	28	39	63	103	192	400	519	4.7	3.6	4.5	6.9
Hispanic	13,641	306	595	1,066	1,754	2,485	4,147	3,172	100.0	100.0	100.0	100.0
Male homosexual/bisexual	6,352	137	289	542	893	1,250	1,747	1,440	46.6	48.6	42.1	45.4
Intravenous drug use	4,900	113	223	385	612	823	1,620	1,085	35.9	37.5	39.1	34.2
Male homosexual/bisexual and intravenous drug use	783	31	47	70	97	148	232	141	5.7	7.9	5.6	4.4
Hemophilia/coagulation disorder	65	1	4	7	5	11	22	15	0.5	0.7	0.5	0.5
Born in Caribbean/African countries	10	—	—	—	3	3	3	3	0.1	—	0.1	0.1
Heterosexual[d]	600	11	18	26	77	100	205	161	4.4	3.0	4.9	5.1
Sexual contact with intravenous drug user	506	10	16	23	69	79	173	134	3.7	2.7	4.2	4.2
Transfusion	186	2	2	7	19	44	64	48	1.4	0.3	1.5	1.5
Undetermined[e]	745	11	12	29	51	106	254	279	5.5	2.0	6.1	8.8

aIncludes cases prior to 1983.

bData are as of September 30, 1989, and reflect reporting delays.

cIncludes all other races not shown separately.

dIncludes persons who have had heterosexual contact with a person with human immunodeficiency virus (HIV) infection or at risk of HIV infection.

eIncludes person for whom risk information is incomplete (because of death, refusal to be interviewed, or loss to followup), persons still under investigation, men reported only to have heterosexual contact with prostitutes, and interviewed persons for whom no specific risk is identified.

Notes: The AIDS case definition was changed in September 1987 to allow for the presumptive diagnosis of AIDS-associated diseases and conditions and to expand the spectrum of HIV-associated diseases reportable as AIDS. Excludes residents of U.S. territories.

Source: National Center for Health Statistics. (1990). *Health United States, 1989.* DHHS Pub. No. 90-1232. Hyattsville, MD: Public Health Services.

Table 6-8

Acquired Immunodeficiency Syndrome (AIDS) Deaths, by Age, Sex, and Race/Ethnicity, Selected Years, 1982 to 1988

Characteristics	Number of Deaths, by Year of Death					Percent Distribution				
	All Years[a]	1982	1984	1986	1988	All Years[a]	1982	1984	1986	1988
Total[b]	43,790	431	3,812	10,010	9,657	100.0	100.0	100.0	100.0	100.0
Whites	25,663	210	1,812	6,025	5,659	58.6	48.7	58.0	60.2	58.6
Minority[c]	18,127	221	1,310	3,985	3,998	41.4	51.3	42.0	38.9	41.4
Blacks	12,257	147	846	2,604	2,861	28.0	34.1	27.1	26.0	29.6
Hispanics	5,503	72	435	1,305	1,044	12.6	16.7	13.9	13.0	10.8
Other races	357	2	29	76	93	0.8	0.5	0.9	0.8	1.0
Males:										
13 years and over[b]	39,551	384	2,849	9,107	8,651	100.0	100.0	100.0	100.0	100.0
White	24,408	197	1,751	5,765	5,354	61.7	51.3	61.5	63.3	61.9
Minority[c]	15,143	187	1,098	3,342	3,297	38.3	48.7	38.5	36.7	38.1
Black	9,957	121	691	2,123	2,294	25.2	31.5	24.3	23.3	26.5
Hispanic	4,861	65	380	1,154	920	12.3	16.9	13.3	12.7	10.6
Other races	325	1	27	65	83	0.8	0.3	0.9	0.7	1.0
Females:										
13 years and over[b]	3,542	36	228	767	870	100.0	100.0	100.0	100.0	100.0
White	1,072	9	53	230	263	30.3	25.0	23.2	30.0	30.2
Minority[c]	2,470	27	175	537	607	69.7	75.0	76.8	70.0	69.8
Black	1,932	20	129	408	496	54.5	55.6	56.6	53.2	57.0
Hispanic	505	6	44	120	103	14.3	16.7	19.3	15.6	11.8
Other races	33	1	2	9	8	0.9	2.8	0.9	1.2	0.9
Children:										
Under 13 years[b]	697	11	45	136	136	100.0	100.0	100.0	100.0	100.0
White	183	4	8	30	42	26.3	36.4	17.8	22.1	30.9
Minority[c]	514	7	37	106	94	73.7	63.6	82.2	77.9	69.1
Black	368	6	26	73	71	52.8	54.5	57.8	53.7	52.2
Hispanic	137	1	11	31	21	19.7	9.1	24.4	22.8	15.4
Other races	9	0	0	2	2	1.3	0.0	0.0	1.5	1.5

[a]Includes death during 1982 through 1988, as well as deaths prior to 1982.
[b]Includes all other races not shown separately.
[c]Category includes blacks, Hispanics, and others.

Notes: Excludes residents of U.S. territories.

Source: National Center for Health Statistics. (1989). *Health, United States, 1988.* Hyattsville, MD: Public Health Services.

dition is a lower level of knowledge about AIDS transmission and prevention. Another is the high rate of street IV drug users among blacks–in comparison to whites (U.S. Department of Health and Human Services, 1985). In addition, few existing black community organizations devote much effort toward AIDS prevention. This lack of attention might result in part from a disproportionate burden of crime on these communities by drug users seeking money for drugs. It has been suggested that the impact of such crime causes these communities to be unfriendly to drug users and less inclined to offer them assistance (Friedman, Sotheran, Abdul-Quader, Primm, Des Jarlais, Kleinman, Mauge, Goldsmith, El-Sadr, and Mashansky, 1989).

AIDS is yet another social ill that afflicts African-Americans disproportionately as a function of their relative status in society. AIDS among blacks is found predominantly among those who are poor, less educated, and less employed (Duh, 1991). We have mentioned above the association between high intravenous drug use among blacks and the prevalence of AIDS among that population. It is not the drug use but the sharing of needles that facilitates HIV transmission; and the sharing of needles is a function of socioeconomic status (Duh, 1991).

Contributing factors to AIDS development are old enemies of black communities: social disruption, a weakened black education system, a weakened black economy, and unhealthy environmental conditions (Duh, 1991; McBride, 1991). Conquering these enemies will contribute significantly to the effort to conquer AIDS.

Other Sexually-Transmitted Diseases

While AIDS might currently be the most serious of the sexually-transmitted diseases (STDs), as no cure has been developed for it, there is cause for concern over a recent increase in the prevalence of other STDs. Reported cases of syphilis, for example, declined from an all-time high of 575,000 cases in 1943 to fewer than 68,000 cases in 1985. However, during the late 1980s there was a substantial increase in infectious syphilis; and most of this increase occurred in low-income, inner-city, minority populations (National Center for Health Statistics, 1990).

Black and Hispanic youths in Massachusetts have an infection rate for sexually transmitted disease that is up to 100 times that of white youths. A statewide survey in 1990 of youth aged 10 to 19 found that the rate of STDs had increased 10.8% over the rate in 1989, which itself was an increase of 15% over the 1988 rate. Black males had a gonorrhea rate more than 100 times the white rate, up from a 65-fold disparity in 1989; and black females had a syphilis rate more than 48 times the white rate, up from a 39-fold disparity in 1989.

As a result of the concern about AIDS and HIV (human immunodeficiency virus) infections, expanded sex education curricula have been developed. However, a 1988 survey of teenagers reported that only 77% reported having received STD education by age 18. In addition, these teenagers had very low awareness of STD symptoms and of approaches to prevention (National Center for Health Statistics, 1990).

Obviously, a critical need is to increase the level of awareness of these issues among all youth.

All STDs, including HIV infection, are historically, biologically, behaviorally, and economically related (Gates and Hinman, 1991). Intimate sexual contact is the common mode of transmission. Also, ulcerative STDs (syphilis, chancroid, and herpes) are associated with increased risk of acquiring and transmitting HIV; and STDs that cause discharge (gonorrhea, chlamydial infection) enhance HIV transmission. Consequently, efforts to prevent HIV infection are being included in efforts to control the spread of STDs. Such efforts include peer-based community education, which has had some success in preventing the spread of AIDS among homosexual men (Gates & Hinman, 1991).

Health Behaviors and Social Structure

The use of illicit drugs by American youth is one of the "problem behaviors" associated with background (i.e., sex, age, parental education and employment status, and family income) and lifestyle status (i.e., dropping out of school, sexual activity). Black youth more often than white youth occupy those status categories that are more closely associated with problem behaviors. Nevertheless, recent data from the National Household Survey on Drug Abuse confirm earlier findings that black youth (ages 10 to 19) are less likely than white or Hispanic youth ever to use cigarettes, alcohol, marijuana, cocaine, and most other illicit drugs (Wallace and Bachman, 1991).

Wallace and Bachman's study suggests that if black and Hispanic youth were as likely as white youth to have highly educated parents, to live with both parents, and to live outside of large urban areas, their levels of use for a number of drugs would be even lower than reported. In seeking to understand what factors ameliorate the relationship between disadvantaged backgrounds and drug use among black youth these authors found religious commitment to be a factor. Black youth are generally more strongly committed to religion than white youth, and they are more likely than white youth to belong to fundamentalist religious dominations, which are seen as major forces in the relative abstinence among blacks.

Although the preceding discussion indicates less abuse of such drugs as cigarettes and alcohol among black youth than among white youth, it would appear that among adults the very opposite situation obtains.[1] More black adults than white adults smoke, although white smokers are heavier smokers (see table 6-1); and blacks suffer from more alcohol-related causes of mortality (see table 6-4).

These higher rates of smoking and alcohol abuse among blacks represent a great shift in the social distribution of these behaviors. Until the 1950s fewer blacks smoked than whites and they had lower levels of deaths from cirrhosis of the liver, a possible indicator of alcohol abuse. Such unhealthy behaviors are often viewed as matters of choice. They are treated as if they are unrelated to working and living conditions and blamed on unhealthy lifestyles on the part of the individuals most affected (Williams, 1990).

We discuss elsewhere in this volume some of the health hazards of workplace environments. Here we wish to make note of some social processes that undoubtedly affect the use of tobacco and alcohol by blacks. One issue for the entire U.S. population is, of course, federal government support. The price support program for tobacco farmers makes tobacco the highest dollar yield per acre of any crop grown in the United States (Williams, 1990). The contradictions between this program and government attention to the health risks posed by tobacco use are often discussed but with little effect.

Government policies also control the availability of alcohol. It is well known that there are more retail liquor stores in black and poor neighborhoods than in more affluent areas. Retail outlets for alcoholic beverages are licensed in every state; and there is a positive association between the availability of alcohol and its consumption (Williams, 1990).

It is also well known that alcohol and tobacco interests push their products to black communities. For example, a large proportion of the billboards for these products are located in black communities. The planned campaign of the R.J. Reynolds Tobacco Company to market a cigarette, Uptown, aimed at blacks is an example of this marketing. Another example was the G. Heileman Brewing Company's Power Master malt liquor, which had 31% more alcohol than that company's topselling Colt 45 brand. Uptown cigarettes and Power Master malt liquor were both pulled from the market after protests by federal government officials and public complaints (*New York Times*, 1991; Palmer, 1991).

A major hindrance to public health efforts to reduce the levels of alcohol and tobacco usage are the financially-based public relations campaigns of these industries. The alcohol industry, for example, even provides financial support to Mothers Against Drunk Drivers and Students Against Drunk Drivers; and the alcohol and tobacco companies contribute heavily to key legislative leaders and members of the U.S. Congress. They also contribute substantially to various ethnic associations, including the black and Hispanic congressional caucuses, the National Urban League, and the United College Fund (Williams, 1990). Possibly, as a result of such contributions these groups do not make formal statements against the efforts of these industries to sell increasing amounts of their products to minority communities.

Summary and Conclusions

African-Americans are at greater risk from each of the modern plagues discussed in this chapter–the direct result of their position in the social structure. A larger proportion of black males smoke than white males, while the trend away from smoking is greater among whites. Each of these phenomena is a function of socioeconomic status.

Blacks drink alcoholic beverages less often than whites. On the other hand blacks have higher alcohol-related morbidity and mortality, a possible result of the difference in career drinking patterns between blacks and whites. Whites tend to be heavy alcohol drinkers at young ages while blacks tend to become heavy drinkers in later adult years. This suggests different motivating factors for drinking, and therefore the need for different methods of prevention. The good news is that alcohol consumption rates are declining. However, the social conditions that may drive black adults to drink heavily are not improving.

AIDS affects blacks disproportionately to their numbers in the population, and the disparity is increasing. Significantly, one of the fastest growing segments of the population to be affected by AIDS is black children who are infected by their infected mothers at birth. Despite the tremendous burden of this disease in black communities, these communities are being criticized by some observers for not mounting more community efforts toward prevention as well as treatment. However, there are several factors affecting the response of black communities to AIDS. These factors include the communities' distrust of the medical establishment, the original stigmatization of Haitians as a high risk group, and the differential response to black health problems. African-Americans harbor a significant distrust of the medical establishment; the infamous Tuskegee syphilis experiment is one concrete example of why such distrust exists.

The differential governmental/societal response to black health problems is exemplified by the fact that $2.5 million in government funds were earmarked for hemophiliacs–a high risk but predominantly white group–because of blood transfusions before the implementation of screening blood supplies for the AIDS virus. Yet, although many persons with sickle cell anemia (who number two-and-one-half times the number of hemophiliacs) regularly receive blood transfusions, no such program has been started for them.

Considering the recent tremendous increase in other sexually transmitted diseases among black youth and the high correlation between HIV infection and other STDs, there is a real possibility for explosive increases in AIDS among this population. Therefore, increased attention must be given to AIDS prevention.

Notes

1.   In the first comprehensive study of smoking among U.S. high school students in 1989, the U.S. Centers for Disease Control found that 36% of white seniors smoked compared to only 16% of black students, and while 16% of the white seniors described themselves as frequent smokers only 2% of the black seniors described themselves as such. Reference: *Cleveland Plain Dealer*. (September 13, 1991). 20% of High School Seniors Smoke. P. 8A.

References

Duh, S.V. (1991). *Blacks and AIDS: Causes and Origins*. Newbury Park, CA: Sage Publications.

EVAXX, Inc. (1983). *A Study of Smoking Behavior Among Black Americans*. New York: American Cancer Society.

Friedman, S., Sotheran, J., Abdul-Quader, A., Primm, B., Des Jarlais, D., Kleinman, R., Mauge, C., Goldsmith, D., El-Sadr, W., & Mashansky, R. (1989). The AIDS Epidemic Among Blacks and Hispanics. In D.P. Willis, *Health Policies and Black Americans*. New Brunswick, NJ: Transaction Publishers.

Gates, W., & Hinman, A.R. (1991). Sexually Transmitted Diseases in the 1990s. *The New England Journal of Medicine, 325* (19), 1368-1369.

Herd, D. (1986). A Review of Drinking Patterns and Problems Among U.S. Blacks. In *Secretary's Task Force on Black and Minority Health, Volume 3: Chemical Dependency and Diabetes*. Washington, DC: U.S. Government Printing Office.

McBride, A.D. (1991). A Perspective on AIDS: A Catastrophic Disease but a Symptom of Deeper Problems in the Black Community. In R. Staples (Ed.), *The Black Family*. Belmont, CA: Wadsworth.

National Center for Health Statistics. (1990). *Health, United States, 1989*. DHHS Pub. No. 90-1232. Public Health Service. Washington, DC: U.S. Government Printing Office.

New York Times. (1991, July 5). U.S. Blocks Power Master. P. D5.

Palmer, T. (1991, July 15). A Target-Marketing Play Backfires. *Boston Globe*.

U.S. Department of Health and Human Services. (1986). *Secretary's Task Force on Black and Minority Health. Volume 3: Chemical Dependency and Diabetes*. Washington, DC: U.S. Government Printing Office.

U.S. Department of Health and Human Services (1990). *Health Status of the Disadvantaged*. DHHS Pub. No. (HRSA) HRS-P-DV 90-1. Public Health Services. Washington, DC: U.S. Government Printing Office.

Wallace, J.M., Jr., & Bachman, J.G. (1991). Explaining Racial/Ethnic Differences in Adolescent Drug Use: The Impact of Background and Lifestyle. *Social Problems, 28* (3), 333-358.

Williams, D.R. (1990). Social Structure and the Health Status of Black Males. *Challenge 1* (1).

7

Sickle Cell Anemia

Sickle cell anemia is a serious morbidity and mortality problem for African-Americans. It manifests itself during the first year of life and usually leads to a difficult childhood and poor prospects for survival into adulthood. At any given time over 50,000 Americans–including 1 in every 400 black Americans–have sickle cell anemia. Those afflicted have a less than 50% chance of living beyond their twentieth birthday; and until recent years few people with the disease lived past their fortieth birthday (Linde, 1972).

Much is known about the sickle cell and the sickling process. However, researchers have not yet developed a cure for the disease that this sickling causes: sickle cell anemia. Sickle cell disease is a critical problem because so many people are afflicted by it. While most genetic diseases affect only a small number of persons, the population of persons with sickle cell anemia is quite large, as shown above.

Sickle cell disease is a genetic disorder in which the red blood cells lose oxygen and assume an elongated shape that resembles a sickle. It is not contagious; it is hereditary. Sickled blood cells tend to cling together; as a result they sometimes clog arteries and veins in the body, cutting off oxygen to vital organs. When blood vessels in the hands and feet get clogged, for instance, the hands and feet become painful and swollen. When blood flow is blocked to such vital organs as the kidneys, the lungs, or the brain, serious damage can occur.

The disease occurs in nearly every country of the world, but it is found most commonly in Africa, the United States, Greece, Italy and other Mediterranean countries, India, countries of Central and South America, and the Caribbean Islands. It occurs mostly in blacks, but has also been found in Puerto Ricans, Indians, Greeks, Turks, Italians, and other whites (Linde, 1972).

Sickle cell disease occurs in two forms–mild or severe. In the mild form the individual rarely suffers any effects from the disease. In the severe form–sickle cell anemia–the individual is usually debilitated, suffers periods of critical illness, and has a shortened life expectancy. Persons with the mild form of the disease have the sickle cell trait, which they inherited from one of their parents and which they will pass on to 50% of any offspring. Persons with the severest form of the disease also inherited the trait from their mother and father. When both parents have the trait, one of four offspring will be normal, one of four will have sickle cell anemia, and two of four will have the trait.

Symptoms

About two-thirds of sickle cell disease patients suffer from periodic painful crises that are thought to be caused by tissue injury resulting from the obstruction of blood flow by the sickled cells (Platt et al., 1991). These painful events usually last from four to six days; yet they may last for weeks, and some patients are always in pain (Charache, Lubin, & Reid, 1985).

Infection, fever, acidosis, dehydration, and exposure to extreme cold may precipitate these painful events. In addition anxiety, depression, and physical exhaustion may precipitate a pain crisis. Between 8% and 10% of patients with sickle cell disease develop leg ulcers, with ulcers appearing more frequently on males than on females (Charache et al., 1985).

A Survey of Persons with Sickle Cell Anemia

In 1984 a survey of clients served in programs supported by the Central Maryland Committee on Sickle Cell Anemia (CMC) was conducted to answer the following questions: Who are the clients? How are clients getting along? What are the major problems that concern the clients? And what kind of (additional) services do the clients want? Respondents were solicited indirectly through five CMC funded programs that serve sickle cell clients in the Baltimore area. Overall, data were collected on 133 clients, including 75 persons who are 18 years of age or older and 58 individuals less than 18 years of age (Reed, 1984).

Adult Clients

In the sample of clients 18 years of age or older, virtually equally divided into males and females, some had not completed high school (see table 7-1). The majority of clients (84%) had no spouse. Nearly two-thirds of the adult clients had never married, and only 16% were currently married.

The employment situation of sickle cell clients is generally problematic: only one-fourth of those surveyed worked full time and only one-third worked at all. Nearly one-third were classified as disabled–which does have a potentially positive side in that such persons may qualify for disability benefits. On the other hand, one-fourth were unemployed or laid off, presumably able to work.

Most of the clients were poor. Over one-half (52%) had a total 1983 family income of less than $8,000. This statistic is made all the more critical when the number of persons supported by the family income is considered. The lower income households in the study had disproportionately more members to support than the higher income households. For example, 41% shared less than $8,000 with one or more other persons and 28% shared $8,000 with two or more persons.

Table 7-1

Sociodemographic Characteristics of Clients 18 + Years of Age

Characteristic	N	Percent
Sex		
Male	38	50.7%
Female	39	49.3
Age		
18 - 21	10	13.3
22 - 30	29	38.7
31 - 40	24	32.0
41 - 50	7	9.3
51 +	5	6.7
Education		
0-8 years	5	6.6
9-11 years	16	21.3
High school graduate	34	45.3
Some college	18	24.0
College graduate	2	2.7
Marital status		
Married	12	16.0
Separated	8	10.7
Widowed	3	4.0
Divorced	5	6.7
Never married	47	62.7
Family income		
$ 8,000	39	52.0
$ 8,000 - 15,000	19	25.3
$ 15,000 +	10	13.3
Not ascertained	7	9.3
Employment		
Working full-time	18	24.0
Working part-time	8	10.7
Retired	1	1.3
Temporarily	2	2.7
Disabled	23	2.7
Unemployed	16	21.3
Housewife	1	1.3
Unable to work	4	5.3
Not ascertained	2	2.7

N = 75

Source: All tables in this chapter were created by the author, using statistics
          gathered in a 1984 survey conducted by the author.

Employment Experience

Only about one-third of the clients were working full or part time, and nearly as many were classified as disabled. Of those persons not working, nearly 90% said that they "would like to have a job." On the other hand, less than half of those who wanted to work felt that they could actually hold a job because of their state of health. Over 30% of those not working had tried a job training program, and most had completed the programs. Only 5%, however, had subsequently obtained a job for which they had been trained.

Some individuals had not worked in a number of years. The overall average time since the last job for those not working was 4.7 years; yet only 20% of the sample was on welfare.

One-third of the working clients had problems with absenteeism from work because of their health. Of the clients currently working, most (72%) had employers who knew that the client had sickle cell anemia. A few of the working clients felt that they are treated unfairly because of their disease. This is only a small proportion of the workers, but it is a problem nevertheless.

Attitudes Toward Illness

Clients were asked "how (they) feel deep down inside about (their) disease?" The wide range of responses to this question are summarized into ten categories in table 7-2. Nearly one-half of the subjects answered that they do not have severe symptoms and/or that they have "learned to live with it." On the other hand, the other half said that they are quite seriously affected by it. They responded that they feel bad about their disease, and they do not appear to be coping very well.

Problems of Clients

Table 7-3 shows how clients were distributed across a range of selected concerns by the degree of their concern. The most pressing concern was employment. Some two-thirds of the clients had severe problems with employment (71.6%) or income (62.7%).

Familiarity and Interaction with Other Programs

Since only 60% of clients had heard of the CMC, and only 28.4% of the clients had heard of ASSERT (Association for Sickle Cell Services, Education, Research & Treatment), it would appear that clients are less knowledgeable than they should be about various programs.

Clients were, however, highly satisfied with the programs that they had participated in, with the exception of social security insurance. Perhaps this is because of the limited amount of income provided by this program.

Table 7-2

Responses to the Question: "How Do You Feel Deep Down about Your Illness?"

Response	N	Percent
No comment/no response	1	1.4%
Have learned to live with it	26	36.1
Stigma hurts	3	4.2
Awful; terrible	9	12.5
Hate it; it interferes with normal activity	11	15.3
Not very severe	8	11.1
Wish it was not so	5	6.9
Varies; family gives good support	2	2.8
Wishes for a cure	2	2.8
Other	5	6.9
Total	72a	100.0

aThree individuals did not respond to this question.

Table 7-3

Selected Problems of Clients

Concern	Percent by Degree of Problem		
	No Problem	Somewhat of a Problem	Important Problem
Housing	73.3%	16.0%	10.7%
Income (money)	37.3	32.0	30.7
Transportation	56.0	29.3	14.7
Nutrition and food	76.0	14.7	9.3
Employment opportunity	28.4	40.5	31.1
Relationship with other persons your age	89.3	8.0	2.7
Weight or size	68.0	20.0	12.0
Physical appearance	89.3	6.7	4.0

Services Desired

The services most desired by sickle cell clients (i.e., more clients indicated these as needs than any other need) were information referral and sickle cell education. Following closely behind these were job placement and employer education. The clients wanted more information themselves and also wished that relevant others–i.e., employers–had more knowledge about the disease. From the relatively low number of persons who felt that they are discriminated against at work because of their disease, we concluded that the desire for employer education was aimed at making employers more willing to hire persons with sickle cell anemia.

The clients also wanted social and information support. More than two-thirds of the clients said that they would like to be a part of a support or self-help group; and 60% indicated that they would like to participate in group activities.

When clients were asked to indicate their first and second most needed services, medically related assistance–transportation to and from medical appointments and assistance with prescription costs–was most often named. Overall, assistance with prescription cost was the greatest need.

Children and Youth

Table 7-4 shows the demographic characteristics of clients less than 18 years of age. These clients were nearly equally divided by sex and ranged in age from 2 to 17 years, with most clients between 6 and 17 years of age. Table 7-5 provides a description of the family situation of these clients. Nearly one-third (31.1%) of the parents or guardians interviewed had not finished high school. Only 22.4% were currently married; and 41.4% had never been married. Similar to the situation of the adult clients, over half of the families had yearly incomes of less than $8,000.

Problems of Clients

Table 7-6 shows how the parents (or guardians) were distributed across a range of selected concerns by the degree of their concern. The most important problem was transportation, with housing, income, and employment opportunities tying as the next most severe problems. Social concerns, such as the child's physical appearance, weight, or size, were not considered significant problems.

Familiarity and Interaction with Other Programs

Respondents were asked about several selected programs that provide services to persons with sickle cell anemia. They were more aware of the Chronic Health Impaired Program (CHIP); and they were slightly more aware of the League for the

Table 7-4

Sociodemographic Characteristics of Clients
Less Than 18 Years of Age

Characteristics	N	Percent
Sex		
Male	27	46.6%
Female	31	53.4
Age		
2-5	11	19.0
6-12	27	46.6
13-17	20	34.4
Education		
None	13	22.4
1-4 years	20	34.5
5-8 years	16	27.6
9-11 years	7	12.1
13-15 years (some college)	1	1.7
Not ascertained	1	1.7
Total	58	100.0

Table 7-5

Sociodemographic Characteristics of Families
of Clients Less Than 18 Years of Age

Characteristics of Parent/Guardian	N	Percent
Education		
7 - 8 years	3	5.2%
9 - 11 years	15	25.9
High school graduate	22	37.9
Some college	13	22.4
College graduate	5	8.6
Marital status		
Married	13	22.4
Separated	12	20.7
Widowed	1	1.7
Divorced	8	13.8
Never married	24	41.4
Family income		
< $8,000	30	51.7
$8,000 - 15,000	14	24.1
$15,000 +	12	20.7
Not ascertained	2	3.4
Employment status		
Working full-time	28	48.3
Working part-time	4	6.9
Temporarily laid off	1	1.7
Disabled	1	1.7
Unemployed	16	27.6
Housewife or widow	5	8.6
Unable to work	3	5.2
Total	58	100.0

Table 7-6

Selected Problems of Clients

Concern	Percent by Degree of Problem		
	No Problem	Somewhat of a Problem	Important Problem
Housing	77.6%	12.1%	10.3%
Income (money)	51.7	37.9	10.3
Transportation	70.2	15.8	14.0
Nutrition and food	79.3	19.0	1.7
Employment opportunity	62.1	27.6	10.3
Relationship with other persons (child's) age	89.7	8.6	1.7
Their weight or size	69.0	29.3	1.7
Their physical appearance	89.7	8.6	1.7

Handicapped. However, they were less aware of several other programs. In general, the users of all of the programs were satisfied with them.

Services Desired

When expressed needs are rank ordered, the greatest overall need was for transportation to and from medical appointments, as over 40% of the parents listed that as their first or second most needed service.

The second greatest overall need was for sickle cell anemia education. Nearly all of the subjects expressed a need for education about the disease. Some of this expressed need may reflect the desire of respondents to have more persons in society–in addition to themselves–educated about the disease. On the other hand, much of this felt need is for more information for themselves, since another important need they expressed is for more information referral services.

The third most frequently stated need is for scholarships. This undoubtedly is a reflection of both the low income level of many of the families and their dissatisfaction with the local public schools, as nearly two-thirds of parents wanted tutoring for their children.

Finally, nearly two-thirds (61.4%) of the parents surveyed expressed a need for a self-help group. We may conclude, then, that some of the greatest needs of families with sickle cell children are informational and educational in nature. Other needs, such as transportation, reflect the low income level of the parents.

Survey Summary

Significantly, the adult clients as well as the families of the children and youths were poor. This situation is underscored by the fact that so few of the family heads had spouses. While one might have expected many of the adult clients not to have married, this would not be the expectation for the mothers of young sickle cell clients.

The situation was a little different in terms of employment. Nearly one-half of the parents of youths were employed full-time as compared to less than one-fourth of the adult clients. A significant number of these employed persons were "working poor," however, as over one-half of their family incomes fell below $8,000 per year.

Many of the adult clients who were not working said that they would like to work if they could get suitable positions. In some cases that would mean almost any kind of job; for others it would require a job within certain constraints in terms of physical exertion, or simply an understanding and sympathetic supervisor.

Many of the clients were getting along quite well with their illness. These individuals either did not have symptoms or had "learned to live" with the disease. Other clients were not so well situated. Many were affected quite seriously both emotionally and physically. More attention should be given to ministering to the psychosocial aspects of the lives of these adult clients.

Overall, clients and parents were not very familiar with the various programs that could be of help to them. Consequently, some kind of information referral service would be extremely useful. Perhaps this can be accomplished through the establishment of mutual support groups. Most adult clients receive requisite help from their informal support network when they are sick; however, many clients could use more information and more intangible services.

The clients in this sample are not necessarily representative of all persons with sickle cell disease; they may be representative only of persons in the types of programs from which they were recruited for the study. It is likely, for instance, that these clients have a lower socioeconomic status than the general population of persons with sickle cell anemia in the United States. On the other hand, the problems and the perspectives of these clients would undoubtedly be representative of a large portion of the sickle cell population. Consequently, their responses can be helpful in understanding the situations of persons with sickle cell.

Management and Therapy

There is currently no known cure for sickle cell anemia. Consequently, appropriate responses to the disease–in addition to working for a cure–include counseling to have patients understand the disease and how to adjust their lifestyle to the disease, and management and therapy for the disease. For example, adults with sickle cell anemia are counseled to seek sedentary occupations and those that offer the best medical allowances. Schools are asked to shield sickle cell students from cold weather, competitive sports, long walks, and heavy stair climbing–all of which tend to bring on sickle cell crises.

The management of sickle cell disease involves education, counseling, prevention, social services, vocational guidance, and clinical support between periods of crisis as well as during crises. In addition to genetic counseling, patients also often require psychological counseling to minimize their feelings of depression about the disease. Such feelings can aggravate their problems (Linde, 1972).

The treatment for pain crises usually consists of hydration (to reverse dehydration), pain relief through the use of analgesics, and the identification and treatment of any precipitating or associated events (Charache et al., 1985).

A recent study has suggested that the medical treatment of sickle cell crises may actually prolong the life of patients. In this decade-long study of several thousand sickle cell patients, medical researchers found that the "pain rate" (number of episodes per year) is a measure of the severity of the disease as it correlates with early death in patients over the age of 20. Thus treatment to reduce the number of crisis episodes will prolong their life (Platt et al., 1991).

Since no specific and definitive therapy for sickle cell anemia currently exists, a number of experimental treatments have been developed. One of these new experimental treatments, the use of the drug hydroxyurea, has begun to show promise. In preliminary studies this drug, which is widely used in the treatment of leukemia, has been shown to reduce the anemia and prevent the pain associated with the disease (Rodgers, 1991). This experimental drug treatment may be the first to affect the disease itself rather than just the symptoms.

These two developments–the potential efficacy of the experimental drug and the importance of reducing the number of pain episodes–combine to suggest promise of real relief to persons with sickle cell disease.

Summary and Conclusion

Despite these promising breakthroughs, sickle cell disease remains a significant morbidity and mortality problem. It affects a large number of people, including 1 out of every 400 black babies. Comparing this figure to other diseases, sickle cell anemia occurs six times more often in blacks than diabetes does in the general population of the United States. It occurs seven times more often than leukemia or cystic fibrosis. In comparing deaths, in Great Britain one out of every 20,000 newborn babies eventually dies from childhood leukemia; in the African Congo death from sickle cell anemia occurs in one of every 100 babies born (Linde, 1972).

During the 1960s and 1970s a number of sickle cell clinics and programs were established to test individuals for the disease, to counsel clients, and to provide assistance with management and therapy. Useful as they are, these clinics are not enough. Sickle cell anemia is not a rare disease, thus much more attention should be given to it. A disease with this large an impact should command more medical research into cures or definitive therapy.

References

Charache, S., Lubin, B., & Reid, C. D. (1985). *Management and Therapy of Sickle Cell Disease.* DHHS (NIH) Pub. No. 85-2117. Public Health Service. Washington, DC: U.S. Government Printing Office.

Linde, S. M. (1972). *Sickle Cell: A Complete Guide to Prevention and Treatment.* New York: Pavilion Publishing.

Platt, O. S., Thorington, B. D., Brambilla, D. J., Milner, P. F., Rosse, W. F., Vichinsky, E., & Kinney, T. R. (1991). Pain in Sickle Cell Disease–Rates and Risk Factors. *The New England Journal of Medicine, 325* (1), 11-16.

Reed, W. L. (1984). *A Survey of Sickle-Cell Clients in CMC Programs.* IUR Report #12. Baltimore: Institute for Urban Research, Morgan State University.

Rodgers, G. P. (1991). Recent Approaches to the Treatment of Sickle Cell Anemia. *Journal of the American Medical Association, 265* (16), 2097-2101.

8

Access to Medical Care

The preceding chapters have discussed the critical health status situation of African-Americans. The other side of the health status "coin" is medical care for health problems. The relative use of such medical care is assessed by examining health services utilization, which is traditionally measured by use of services such as ambulatory care and hospital care. These services may be further delineated by the types of services provided, such as preventive care, education, and diagnostic and treatment procedures, as well as by the continuity of these treatments. Access to health care usually comes through a family physician or a hospital outpatient department. More seriously ill persons may be referred to specialists or to hospitals by their primary care provider. Hospital care is generally measured by such indicators as admission rates and length of stay.

If both the incidence of disease rates and access to the health care system were equal for different groups of people, we could expect health services utilization rates to be equal. As has been observed in other chapters of this volume, however, there are significant differences in life expectancy and morbidity and mortality rates between black Americans and white Americans. This would imply that those groups experiencing higher morbidity and mortality rates should be using more health services. For example, among the chronically ill we would expect to find more ambulatory care visits, and among the seriously ill, higher hospitalization rates.

Between 1985 and 1987, the total U.S. population, as reported in the National Center for Health Statistics' National Health Interview Survey (1990), visited physicians an average of 5.3 times per year (see table 8-1). Annual visits by blacks and whites were very different, however, with whites having 17% more visits per person. White children (under 18 years of age) had an average of 1.7 more physician visits each year than black children, while blacks 18 and over more closely approximated the average number of physician contacts by whites over most categories of sex, income, poverty status, employment status, and education. Persons having family incomes under $10,000 a year average over one-and-a-half (1.6) more visits each year than those with incomes of $35,000 or more, a function undoubtedly of the generally poorer health of poor persons.

Table 8-1

Average Annual Number of Physician Contacts Per Person, by Age, Race, Family Income, Education, and Employment Status, 1985-87

Characteristics	All Ages			Under 18 Years		18-44 Years		45-64 Years		65 Years and Over	
	All Races	White	Black	White	Black	White	Black	White	Black	White	Black
Total	5.3	5.5	4.7	4.5	2.8	4.7	4.5	6.3	7.1	8.8	8.7
Sex											
Male	4.5	4.6	3.9	4.5	2.9	3.4	3.3	5.4	6.4	8.3	8.1
Female	6.2	6.3	5.4	4.5	2.8	6.0	5.5	7.2	7.7	9.2	9.1
Family income											
Less than $10,000	6.7	7.2	5.5	4.4	3.2	6.1	5.5	10.3	9.4	9.6	9.1
$10,000 - $19,999	5.5	5.6	4.6	4.1	2.5	4.7	4.9	7.2	6.5	8.4	8.9
$20,000 - $34,999	5.1	5.3	4.3	4.7	2.8	4.7	4.1	6.1	6.9	8.6	8.2
$35,000 or more	5.1	5.2	4.6	5.0	3.3	4.7	4.9	5.6	5.5	9.3	7.4
Poverty status											
In poverty	5.7	6.1	5.0	3.9	3.1	5.9	5.2	10.7	9.5	9.7	10.3
Not in poverty	5.4	5.5	4.7	4.7	2.8	4.7	4.6	6.2	6.5	8.8	8.1
Employment status											
Employed	4.5	4.6	4.3	—	—	4.2	4.0	5.1	5.1	7.5	4.8
Unemployed	4.7	4.7	4.5	—	—	4.7	3.9	4.8	7.6	4.8	9.8
Not in labor force	8.3	8.4	8.4	—	—	6.9	6.4	8.9	10.6	9.0	9.3
Education											
Less than 12 years	6.5	6.6	6.5	—	—	4.5	4.2	6.8	7.9	8.6	8.6
12 years	5.5	5.6	4.8	—	—	4.6	4.2	6.2	6.4	8.6	8.1
More than 12 years	5.6	5.6	5.6	—	—	4.9	5.1	6.2	6.3	9.2	11.3

Source: Ries, P.W. (1990). *Health of Black and White Americans 1985-87*. National Center for Health Statistics. Vital Health Statistics. Series 10, No. 171. Public Health Service. Washington, DC: U.S. Government Printing Office.

Utilization of Medical Services

Physician Visits

The settings within which physician contacts take place are generally different for whites and blacks. Over 60% of the visits made by whites in 1988 took place in a physician's office (60.6%), compared to only 49% by blacks (see table 8-2). Whites were nearly twice as likely to consult physicians over the telephone as were blacks (14.4% to 8.6%). Over 20% of the physician contacts made by blacks occurred in hospital clinics or emergency rooms (21.5%), compared to only 11.8% by whites. Except for the large increase in the percentage of home visits (which, overall, account for a very small percentage of contacts) the only place that blacks increased their usage between 1983 and 1988 was in physician office visits.

Income is also related to place of physician visit: the higher the income level, the higher the proportion of visits that take place in physicians' offices and the higher the rate of telephone consultations; the lower the income, the higher the proportion of visits that take place in hospital settings (see table 8-2). Given that a larger proportion of minority individuals than whites are poor, we may infer that hospital outpatient departments are used as a source of first contact with medical care by a disproportionate number of low-income blacks and other minorities.

As the above observation suggests, blacks and other nonwhites make fewer office visits to physicians–and they are losing ground. Table 8-3 lists the average number of office visits made by whites and people of other races in 1980 and 1985. The rate for nonwhites went down during this period, from 2.03 to 1.94, for all specialties, while the rate for whites went up, from 2.73 to 2.84. While the white rate held fairly steady for internal medicine visits and obstetric and gynecological visits, the nonwhite rate went down; and perhaps more ominously, while whites increased their office visits to pediatricians, nonwhites decreased their usage. General surgery visits was the only category to go the other way: the white rate went down slightly, while the nonwhite rate went up.

While the settings within which physician visits take place vary by race and income, the types of services received appear to be very similar for both race and income groups (see table 8-4). About 84% of all physician visits made by all persons involve diagnosis and treatment and about 4% involve a general check-up. These percentages do not vary much by race or income. Blacks actually report that 5% of their visits involve general checkups, which is somewhat higher than the 3.7% reported by whites.

Lower income persons assess their health as being poorer, report greater limitations in their activity, have more days of restricted activity and bed disability due to illness, report more physician visits, and use outpatient departments more often than higher income persons (Ries, 1990; National Center for Health Statistics, 1990). When they see a physician, they report slightly more visits for diagnosis and treatment, and slightly fewer visits for general checkups (see table 8-4).

Table 8-2

Physician Contacts, by Place of Contact, Race, and Income, 1983 and 1988

Percent Distribution

Characteristics	Total	Doctor's Office		Hospital Outpatient Department		Telephone		Home		Other	
		1983	1988	1983	1988	1983	1988	1983	1988	1983	1988
Total	100.0	56.1	59.3	14.9	12.8	15.5	13.7	1.5	1.4	12.0	12.7
Race											
White	100.0	57.6	60.6	13.4	11.8	16.3	14.4	1.5	1.3	11.1	11.9
Black	100.0	44.3	49.3	26.8	21.5	9.7	8.6	1.1	2.3	18.2	18.3
Family income											
Less than $10,000	100.0	49.9	49.4	18.5	19.2	12.4	11.3	1.5	2.1	17.7	18.0
$10,000 - $14,999	100.0	52.3	56.2	17.6	15.1	13.0	12.0	2.0	1.1	15.1	15.6
$15,000 - $19,999	100.0	54.5	58.7	16.7	13.8	16.4	13.7	1.3	1.6	11.1	12.2
$20,000 - $34,999	100.0	59.3	61.7	13.3	10.7	16.2	16.1	0.7	0.8	10.5	10.7
$35,000 or more	100.0	59.7	62.4	11.6	9.3	19.0	15.1	1.1	1.6	8.6	11.6

Source: National Center for Health Statistics. (1990). *Health, United States, 1989*. DHHS Pub. No. (PHS) 90-1232. Hyattsville, MD: Public Health Service.

Table 8-3

Office Visits Per Person to Physicians, According to Physician
Speciality, by Race, 1980 and 1985

Characteristics	1980	1985
All specialties		
White	2.73	2.84
All others	2.03	1.94
General and family practices		
White	0.89	0.84
All others	0.70	0.69
Internal medicine		
White	0.31	0.31
All others	0.24	0.21
Obstetrics and gynecology		
White	0.23	0.22
All others	0.23	0.18
Pediatrics		
White	0.39	0.43
All others	0.25	0.23
General surgery		
White	0.13	0.12
All others	0.08	0.11

Source: National Center for Health Statistics. (1990). *Health, United States, 1989.*
DHHS Pub. No. (PHS) 90-1232. Hyattsville, MD: Public Health Service.

Table 8-4

Percent of Physician Visits, by Type of Service[a], Race, and Income, 1980

Characteristic	All Visits	Type of Services				
		Diagnosis or Treatment	Prenatal & Postnatal Care	General Checkup	Immunization & Vaccination	Other
Total	1,036,092	84.4	8.3	3.9	1.9	3.0
Race						
White	229,732	84.7	8.0	3.7	1.8	3.1
Black	115,496	82.7	9.4	5.0	2.2	2.2
Family income						
Under $10,000	274,134	85.6	7.5	3.0	2.1	2.9
$10,000 - $24,999	408,325	83.1	8.3	4.9	2.3	3.1
$25,000 +	274,755	84.6	8.8	3.4	1.2	3.1

[a]The sum of percent by type of service may be greater than 100.0 because one visit may involve more than one type of service.

Sources: *Physician Visit, Volume & Interval Since Last Visit, United States, 1980.* Data from the National Health Survey Series 10, No. 144. Washington, DC: U.S. Government Printing Office.

Hospital Utilization

Hospital utilization, as measured by the average number of days in the hospital for persons admitted, was found to vary by racial background in the National Health Interview Survey. In 1987 blacks averaged 1.4 more days a year in the hospital than whites (8.0 days versus 6.6 days) (National Center for Health Statistics, 1990).

The average number of hospital days each year is inversely related to family income for both blacks and whites (see table 8-5). Persons residing in households earning less than $20,000 a year averaged nearly 3 (2.7) hospital days more than do those from households earning $20,000 or more a year, a probable function of the association of socioeconomic status and health. While age is positively related to the average number of days spent in the hospital for all groups, blacks spend more days in hospitals than whites at each age level. And even when controlling for income, age, or number of episodes, blacks have a greater number of hospital days than whites.

Another source of information on hospitalization is the hospital discharge data. Although all racial/ethnic groups reported in these data were lumped into two categories–white and nonwhite–the category "nonwhite" has been found to be a useful proxy for blacks in other federal surveys. These data indicate that, overall, in 1982 whites averaged slightly shorter lengths of hospital stays than nonwhites: 7.1 days versus 7.2 days (see table 8-6). When looking at selected categories of first-listed diagnoses, nonwhites average longer hospital stays than whites for all neoplasms (an abnormal growth of tissue) and diseases of the circulatory and digestive systems. They average slightly fewer days for diseases of the respiratory system. The rates of patients discharged from short-stay hospitals by race and first-listed diagnosis are also given in table 8-6.

It is not clear that seriously ill low-income or minority persons are taken care of at the place of first medical visit in a manner that would reflect equal access to hospital services. Longer lengths of stay for diseases that are more prevalent in minority populations, coupled with less frequent hospital discharges, usually means that the population is diagnosed at a later stage of the disease–that they are "sicker," and therefore need more hospital care. It is difficult to speculate on the factors that may be at work to keep the discharge rates lower for the serious illnesses that are more prevalent in minority populations. Why are these people not showing up in the hospital discharge statistics? Perhaps they are not discharged. It would appear that a greater proportion of nonwhites die in the hospital.

Health Insurance and Other Third Party Payers

One component of access to health services is the ability to pay. Payment for health services takes place in several ways. Private health insurance usually pays for hospital care, and many private insurance plans also cover some portion of physician services. For those persons over the age of 65 and eligible for Social Security,

Table 8-5

Average Annual Number of Short-Stay Hospital Days Per Person
Hospitalized for All Causes Except Deliveries, by Number of Episodes,
Family Income, Race, and Age, 1985-87

Characteristics	All Episodes	1 Episode	2 Episodes	3 or More Episodes
Family income less than $20,000				
All persons	10.5	7.1	16.8	30.5
White				
All ages	10.3	6.9	16.1	30.1
Under 18 years	6.7	5.0	13.9	22.6
18-44 years	8.3	5.8	13.6	30.4
45-64 years	11.7	7.5	16.0	33.3
65 years and over	12.1	8.2	17.8	29.1
Black				
All ages	11.5	7.9	20.9	33.3
Under 18 years	10.1	6.2	27.9a	40.0a
18-44 years	9.7	7.6	14.8	29.9
45-64 years	13.5	8.3	27.3	33.2
65 years and over	13.5	9.6	19.5	30.9
Family income $20,000 or more				
All persons	7.8	5.4	14.1	27.8
White				
All ages	7.7	5.4	14.1	26.9
Under 18 years	6.2	4.5	15.7	30.5
18-44 years	6.6	4.8	12.8	24.6
45-64 years	8.4	5.7	13.3	27.4
65 years and over	10.5	7.2	16.5	27.7
Black				
All ages	8.6	6.4	15.1	33.1
Under 18 years	7.5	6.2	13.6a	21.3a
18-44 years	7.3	5.5	14.1	28.5a
45-64 years	10.6	7.9	17.4a	34.9a
65 years and over	13.7	9.2a	15.5a	42.3a

a Figure does not meet standard of reliability or precision (more than 30 percent relative standard error in numerator of percent or rate).

Source: Ries, P.W. (1990). *Health of Black and White Americans 1985-87*. National Center for Health Statistics. Vital Health Statistics. Series 10, No. 171. Public Health Service. Washington, DC: U.S. Government Printing Office.

Table 8-6

Rate of Patents Discharged from Short-Stay Hospitals and Average Length of Stay, by Selected Categories of First-Listed Diagnosis and by Race, 1982

Category of First-Listed Diagnosis (and ICD-9-CM Code)	Rate of Patients Discharged Per 10,000 Population			Average Length of Stay in Days		
	All Races	White	All Others	All Races	White	All Others
All conditions	1,679.0	1,518.2	1,555.8	7.1	7.1	7.2
Neoplasms (140-239)	112.8	105.9	90.0	9.9	10.0	10.7
Malignant neoplasms (10-208, 230-234)	85.8	82.4	59.2	11.1	11.1	12.8
Malignant neoplasm of trachea, bronchus and lung (162, 197.0, 197.3)	13.9	13.3	11.1	10.9	10.9	11.6
Malignant Neoplasm of breast (175-175, 198.81)	9.9	9.7	5.4	10.0	9.9	12.7
Benign neoplasm & neoplasms, uncertain behavior & unspecified nature (210-229, 236-239)	27.1	23.6	30.8	6.1	6.1	6.6
Diseases of the circulatory system (390-459)	238.8	228.9	169.5	9.4	9.4	10.3
Diseases of the respiratory system (460-519)	150.5	138.7	127.6	6.2	6.4	5.8
Disease of the digestive system (520-579)	201.3	187.1	162.0	6.8	6.8	7.4
Injury & poisoning (800-899)	155.2	138.5	151.3	7.4	7.5	7.5

Source: *Utilization of Short-Stay Hospital United States, 1982.* Annual Summary Data from the National Health Survey Series 13, No. 78. DHHS Pub. No. (PHS) 84-1739. Washington, DC: U.S. Government Printing Office.

Medicare pays for a major portion of hospital care. Medicare eligibles may also purchase insurance to cover physician services. For selected low-income individuals, the federally subsidized, state administered Medicaid program pays for medical care costs, although in many cases at reduced rates. Persons who have no third party coverage–e.g, poor persons who do not quality for Medicaid–must pay for services out of their own pockets or may become "charity" cases.

In 1985 nearly 87% of the U.S. population reported having some form of health insurance coverage (see table 8-7). However, only 80.7% of blacks reported having insurance coverage. At that time 76.5% of all persons having health insurance were covered by private insurance plans, 7.3% by Medicaid, and 13.3% had no coverage. A much higher proportion of whites than blacks had private sources of insurance, reflecting the much higher employment and income rates among whites.

The trend during the 1980s was one of an increasing proportion of persons having no health insurance coverage. This is the case for both blacks and whites (see table 8-8). Amongst black Americans, Medicaid coverage has held steady or decreased, and the uninsured proportion has increased.

Having health insurance is related to whether or not people report having a usual source of medical care. One-fourth (24.8%) of the medically uninsured report having no usual source of care (table 8-9). This is a higher percentage than for those with private, Medicare, or Medicaid coverage. Having health insurance appears to increase the likelihood of having a usual source of medical care.

When looking at the of usual source of health care as reported in the 1977 National Medical Care Expenditures Study (NMCES) survey, virtually the same high proportions of persons covered by private health insurance or Medicare report the physician's office as their usual source of care: 69.8% and 70.6%, respectively (see table 8-9). However, only 52% of those uninsured or on Medicaid cite a physician's office as the usual place of care. Nearly 12% of those covered by Medicaid report outpatient departments or emergency rooms as their primary sources of care.

While virtually everyone aged 65 and over is covered by Medicare, that program does not provide full insurance coverage for all health needs. In order to fill the gaps in Medicare, people who are able to often obtain private health insurance. Overall, in 1986, 71.6% of this older population had both Medicare and private insurance coverage, whereas 17.9% had Medicare only, and 5.8% had both Medicare and Medicaid (table 8-10). Significantly, whites supplement Medicare with private insurance more than twice as frequently as blacks: 75.4% as opposed to 34.2%. One-fifth (19.7%) of elderly blacks have Medicaid and Medicare and one-third (34.9%) have Medicare only. During the 1980s there was an increase in the proportion of elderly with Medicare and private insurance and a decrease in those with just Medicare or with Medicare and Medicaid.

One of the major gaps in Medicare is coverage for nursing home care. Blacks generally underutilize nursing homes (see table 8-11). When looking at primary sources of nursing home payment by racial/ethnic background, whites are nearly three times as likely as blacks to make payment from their own or family income.

Table 8-7

Health Insurance Coverage, by Sex and Race, 1985

Characteristic	Total	Percent			
		Total	Private	Covered by Medicaid	Not Covered by Health Insurance
Total persons	100.0	86.7%	76.5%	7.3%	13.3%
Sex					
Male	100.0	85.4	76.6	5.6	14.6
Female	100.0	88.0	76.3	8.9	12.0
Race					
White	100.0	87.6	79.6	5.0	12.4
Black	100.0	80.7	55.7	21.6	19.3

Source: Horton, C.P., and Smith, J.C. (1990). *Statistical Record of Black America.* Detroit: Gale Research.

Table 8-8

Health Care Coverage for Persons Under 65 Years of Age,
by Type of Coverage, 1980, 1982, 1986

Characteristic by Year	Black	White	All Races
1980			
Private insurance	60.1%	81.9%	78.8%
Medicaid	17.9	3.9	5.9
Not covered	19.0	11.4	12.5
1982			
Private insurance	59.6%	80.4%	77.3%
Medicaid	17.2	3.6	5.6
Not covered	21.1	13.5	14.7
1986			
Private insurance	57.0%	79.1%	75.9%
Medicaid	17.4	4.0	5.9
Not covered	22.6	14.0	15.3

Note: Percentages do not add up to 100 because the percentages of individuals with other types of health insurance (e.g., Medicare, military) and unknown health insurance are not shown, and because persons with both private insurance and Medicaid appear in both columns.

Source: National Center for Health Statistics. (1990). *Health, United States, 1989*. DHHS Pub. No. (PHS) 90-1232. Hyattsville, MD: Public Health Service.

Table 8-9

Usual Sources of Care: Percent Distribution of Persons, by Insurance Coverage, 1977

Characteristic	Population (in thousands)	No Usual Source	Usual Source of Care				
			Physician's Office	Hospital Outpatient Department	Emergency Room	Health Center/ Other	Don't Know/ No Answer
Insurance Coverage							
Private	170,329%	13.3%	69.8%	3.0%	0.8%	4.0%	9.1%
Medicare	24,122	10.8	70.6	5.7	0.7	4.0	8.2
Medicaid	22,752	15.0	52.2	9.6	2.3	10.3	10.6
Uninsured	16,569	24.8	51.5	6.4	1.4	6.1	9.8

Source: National Center for Health Services Research. (1982). *Usual Sources of Medical Care & Their Characteristics*, Data Preview, 12. NCHSR National Medical Care Expenditures Study. DHHS Pub. No. (PHS) 82-3324. Washington, DC: U.S. Government Printing Office.

Table 8-10

Health Care Coverage for Persons Over 65 Years of Age, by Type of Coverage, 1980, 1982, 1986

Characteristic by Year	Black	White	All Races
1980			
Medicare and private insurance	26.5%	68.3%	64.4%
Medicare and Medicaid	23.3	6.6	8.1
Medicare only	40.6	21.0	22.7
1982			
Medicare and private insurance	33.0%	68.9%	65.5%
Medicare and Medicaid	18.2	4.8	6.1
Medicare only	38.5	21.6	23.1
1986			
Medicare and private insurance	34.2%	75.4%	71.6%
Medicare and Medicaid	19.7	4.5	5.8
Medicare only	34.9	16.1	17.9

Source: National Center for Health Statistics. (1990). *Health, United States, 1989.* DHHS Pub. No. (PHS) 90-1232. Hyattsville, MD: Public Health Service.

Table 8-11

Nursing Home and Personal Care Home Residents 65 Years of Age and Over, by Age and Race, 1963, 1973-74, 1977, and 1985

Characteristics	Residents per 1,000 Population			
	1963	1973-74	1977	1985
White	26.6	46.9	48.9	47.7
65-74 years	8.1	12.5	14.2	12.3
75-84 years	41.7	60.3	67.0	59.1
85 years and over	157.7	270.8	234.2	228.7
Black	10.3	22.0	30.7	35.0
65-74 years	5.9	11.1	17.6	15.4
75-84 years	13.8	26.7	33.4	45.3
85 years and over	41.8	105.7	133.6	141.5

Source: National Center for Health Statistics. (1990). *Health, United States, 1989.* DHHS Pub. No. (PHS) 90-1232. Hyattsville, MD: Public Health Service.

Medicaid is the primary source of payment for nearly two-thirds of black nursing home residents (National Center for Health Statistics, 1990).

Medicaid was initiated in 1966 to increase health care utilization by the poor and disadvantaged. Since that time national studies have indicated that utilization rates by the poor have indeed increased. The average number of physician visits made in 1964, 1975, 1980, and 1988 are compared in table 8-12. Although the number of visits increased slightly between 1964 and 1975, and gained between 1980 and 1988, most of the increases in utilization occurred for persons with income under $10,000. Overall, utilization increased by about 17% between 1964 and 1988. However, during the same period persons in families earning less than $10,000 increased their rate by approximately 70%, undoubtedly the result of Medicaid.

Data from the early years of Medicaid indicate that public assistance recipients had higher levels of physician visits, hospital episodes, and hospital days than nonrecipients. However, among all persons receiving public assistance, blacks–particularly those living in the South–had lower utilization rates than whites. Early Medicaid information also indicates that blacks on the average received lower amounts of Medicaid payment than did whites (Davis, 1976).

Health insurance does appear to help equalize access to health services, but as outlined above there are different degrees of insurance coverage, and the equality and scope of coverage tends to influence utilization. As with other things, while large groups of the population are covered by some type of insurance, poorer people are less likely to be covered whether black or white.

Quality of Care

When blacks do utilize available services, their care tends to be episodic. While crude overall utilization statistics reveal few racial disparities, there are marked differences in the location, source, and quality of care for black health care seekers (Link et al., 1982).

Recent data indicate an average annual rate of office visits to physicians for coronary heart disease (CHD) in nonwhites that is about half that for whites (42/1,000 versus 80/1,000) (Aday and Andersen, 1984). Office visits of all kinds by black patients were most likely to be to general and family practitioners (46.6%); 10.7% of visits were to internists and 0.8% to cardiovascular disease (CVD) specialists. Black patients are much less likely than white patients to see CVD specialists, which "probably has an adverse effect on the exposure of black patients with CHD to accurate diagnosis and appropriate treatment" (U.S. Department of Health and Human Services, 1985, p. 50). Visits to physicians in hospital clinics and emergency rooms constituted 11.8% of physician visits by whites and 21.5% of physician visits by blacks. In contrast, 60.6% of all visits by whites were to physicians' offices, compared to 49.3% of visits by blacks (table 8-2). Thus, blacks are less likely to have regular family doctors for their health care, than are whites.

Table 8-12

Number of Annual Physician Contacts Per Person, by Race and Income,
1964, 1975, 1980, and 1988

Characteristics	1964	1975	1980	1988
Total	4.6	5.0	4.7	5.4
Race				
White	4.7	5.1	4.8	5.5
Black	3.6	4.9	4.6	5.1
Family income				
Less than $7,000	3.9	5.9	5.5	6.8a
$7,000 - $9,999	4.2	5.2	4.4	6.8a
$10,000 - $14,999	4.7	5.0	4.9	5.6
$15,000 - $24,999	4.8	4.9	4.7	5.2-5.4
$25,000 or more	5.2	5.0	4.6	5.2-5.4

a6.8 Visits per person under $10,000.

Sources: U.S. Department of Health and Human Services. (1985). *Health Status of Minorities and Low Income Groups*. DHHS Pub. No. (HRSA) HRS-P-DV 85-1. Washington, DC: U.S. Government Printing Office; and U.S. Department of Health and Human Services. (1990). *Health Status of the Disadvantaged–Chartbook 1990*. DHHS Pub. No. (HRSA) HRS-P-DV 90-1. Public Health Service. Washington, DC: U.S. Government Printing Office.

It is difficult to assess the quality of medical care that patients receive from providers. Traditional wisdom suggests three approaches: structure, process, and outcome. Outcome is thought to be the ultimate measure; that is, the degree of reduction in morbidity and mortality. The argument goes that if individuals with similar health problems are exposed to different health care systems, then quality of care may be judged by the degree to which their health care system shows minimal rates of morbidity and mortality. The problem, however, is that we have no reliable measures with which to define the health status of individuals as they enter the health care system, or as they emerge from it. We do not even have positive measures of whether or not the health care system has had a chance to play its assigned role of education, prevention, diagnosis, and treatment. So what we do is use other indicators—such as process or structure—as measures of quality of care.

Having a usual source of medical care facilitates health services utilization and is considered desirable. In the 1977 NMCES Survey, 14.2% of the U.S. population reported having no usual source of care. Blacks were more likely to have no usual health care source than whites—19.7% versus 13.1%. These rates increased by 1986 to 20.1% and 16.3%, respectively (see table 8-13). Whites reported physicians' offices as their usual source of care more frequently than either blacks or Hispanics. Having a usual source of care was also related to income. Persons with annual family incomes of $12,000 or more were more likely to report having a usual source of care than persons whose families earned less than $12,000 (National Center for Health Services Research, 1982).

Race was related to the place of usual medical care. Twenty-five percent of blacks reported hospital outpatient departments, emergency rooms, and health centers as their usual source of health care, whereas only 16.6% of whites reported these places as regular sources. Family income was also related to place of care: a larger proportion of lower income persons cited a place other than a physician's office as their usual care source than did upper income persons (National Center for Health Services Research, 1982).

Another measure that is used as an indirect indicator of quality of medical care is the satisfaction level of the client. Very few clients report dissatisfaction with the care they receive (Robert Wood Johnson Foundation, 1987). However, the rate of reported dissatisfaction among blacks is one-and-one-half to two or more times greater than dissatisfaction reported by whites (table 8-13). According to a survey by the Robert Wood Johnson Foundation, 4% of blacks as opposed to 2% of whites were dissatisfied with their ambulatory visits; and 6.1% of blacks compared to 3.8% of whites were dissatisfied with their hospitalization.

Waiting room time is one of several measures used to indicate system responsiveness, and therefore quality of care. The average overall length of time spent waiting for a physician was 29 minutes in the NMCES survey (table 8-14). Nonwhites averaged waiting periods 13 to 25 minutes longer than whites for care, depending upon age. The time spent waiting for physicians was also related to the site of the visits. Both nonwhites and whites spent more minutes waiting for physicians

Table 8-13

Selected Indicators of Access to Medical Care, by Race and Income, 1986

Characteristic	Race		Family Income	
	Black	White	Poor	Non-poor
People without a regular source of care	20.1%	16.3%	20.2%	16.8%
Average number of ambulatory visits	3.4	4.4	4.4	4.4
People who did not have an ambulatory visit in the preceding 12 months	37.4%	31.6%	34.5%	32.1%
Of those who did have at least one ambulatory visit, the proportion not at all satisfied with their most recent visit	4.0%	2.0%	4.5%	1.8%
People hospitalized at least once in the 23 months prior to the survey	6.2%	6.8%	7.9%	6.2%
Of those hospitalized, the proportion not at all satisfied with their most recent hospitalization	6.1%	3.8%	6.6%	3.6%
People with chronic or serious illnesses	21.1%	20.4%	22.7%	18.3%

Source: Robert Wood Johnson Foundation. (1987). *Access to Health Care in the United States: Results of a 1986 Survey.* Princeton, NJ: Author.

Table 8-14

Mean Waiting Time (in Minutes) to See a Physician, by Site of Care, Race, and Age, 1977

Characteristics	All Sites	Physician's Office	Other Sites
Whites			
Below age 65	27.4	26.2	33.1
65+	28.4	28.0	31.4
Nonwhites			
Below age 65	41.0	34.9	53.3
65+	54.1	46.1	81.4
Total	29.1	27.4	37.2

Source: National Center for Health Services Research. (1982). *Usual Sources of Medical Care & Their Characteristics,* Data Preview, 12. NCHSR National Medical Care Expenditures Study. DHHS Pub. No. (PHS) 82-3324. Washington, DC: U.S. Government Printing Office.

at sites other than offices; however, this relationship was much greater for nonwhites than for whites. Among nonwhites, age also appears to be strongly related to waiting time to see physicians. At physicians' offices and other sites of care older nonwhites, 65 and above, waited between 11 and 28 minutes longer than nonwhites under 65.

Use of Services Relative to Need

Since African-Americans are generally in poorer health than whites it is assumed that they require more medical services. Above we have seen that the rates of utilization of medical care services by blacks have been consistently lower than those of whites. In the late 1970s blacks were nearly equal to whites in their rate of physician visits; however, during the 1980s the gap between whites and blacks began to widen (see table 8-12).

To assess the extent to which African-Americans receive needed medical care we can look at utilization relative to medical need. Tables 8-15 and 8-16 examine the use of medical services by a measure of health status. Overall, blacks have significantly fewer visits to physicians. However, the bulk of this disparity is made by the great difference in the number of physician visits by children and youth (those under the age of 18), as black adults have rates of visits that are nearly equal to–and sometimes greater than–those of whites (table 8-15). This age differentiation obtains also in each of the health status categories. In the "good to excellent" health category, among persons less than 18 years old whites have 59% more visits than blacks. This difference is even greater in the "fair or poor health" category; here whites under the age of 18 have nearly two-and-a-half times more visits than blacks.

Blacks spend more days in the hospital per year than whites, a situation that obtains for individuals with either good or poor health status (table 8-16). However, the difference was greater among those with "fair or poor" health.

Equity of access is determined by the degree to which people in need of medical care receive it (Andersen, 1978). When utilization is compared to need, blacks obtain needed care less readily than do whites (Aday & Andersen, 1975; 1984; Health Resources Administration, 1977; Reed, 1984; 1990).

A recent study of the black urban elderly sought to determine whether this group had equity of access to medical services (Reed, 1984). The normed measure of access to medical care used in the study was based on a list of general symptoms of illness. Included in this list were coughs, weakness, excessive fatigue, headaches, rashes, diarrhea, shortness of breath, aching joints, backaches, weight loss, heart pains, and infected eyes or ears. This checklist of symptoms was used to develop a symptoms-response ratio. For each reported symptom respondents were asked whether a physician was seen in response to the symptom. The severity of each symptom was determined for each of five different age groups (1-5, 6-15, 16-44, 45-64, 65 and over) by a panel of forty physicians (see Taylor et al., 1975). The physicians estimated what proportion of individuals in each age group would need to see a physi-

Table 8-15

Average Annual Number of Physician Contacts Per Person, by Race,
Respondent-Assessed Health Status, and Age, 1985-87

Characteristics	Black	White
All health statuses		
All ages	4.7	5.5
Under 18 years	2.8	4.5
18-44 years	4.5	4.7
45-64 years	7.1	6.3
65 years	8.7	8.8
Fair or poor health		
All ages	11.8	14.9
Under 18 years	6.5	15.5
18-44 years	11.2	15.6
45-64 years	13.0	15.1
65 years	13.0	14.4
Good to excellent health		
All ages	3.4	4.5
Under 18 years	2.7	4.3
18-44 years	3.7	4.2
45-64 years	4.2	4.6
65 years	5.0	6.5

Source: Ries, P.W. (1990). *Health of Black and White Americans 1985-87*.
          National Center for Health Statistics. Vital Health Statistics. Series 10,
          No. 171. Public Health Service. Washington, DC: U.S. Government
          Printing Office.

Table 8-16

Average Annual Number of Days in Short-Stay Hospital Per Person
Hospitalized During the Year Preceding Interview, by Race,
Respondent-Assessed Health Status, and Age, 1986-87

Characteristics	Black	White
All health statuses		
All ages	9.5	8.2
Under 18 years	8.8	6.4
18-44 years	7.1	5.9
45-64 years	12.3	9.7
65 years	14.0	11.7
Fair or poor health		
All ages	14.7	13.3
Under 18 years	19.1	12.8
18-44 years	12.0	11.4
45-64 years	15.1	13.7
65 years	15.9	14.0
Good to excellent health		
All ages	6.4	6.3
Under 18 years	6.4	5.7
18-44 years	5.7	5.0
45-64 years	7.8	6.9
65 years	9.8	9.5

Source: Ries, P.W. (1990). *Health of Black and White Americans 1985-87*.
National Center for Health Statistics. Vital Health Statistics. Series 10,
No. 171. Public Health Service. Washington, DC: U.S. Government
Printing Office.

cian for the symptom. Thus these estimates suggest how often care *should* be sought, and this can be compared to how often care *was* sought.

A summary measure of access combines the physicians' judgments and the actual population response. The computational formula is (A-E)/E, where A equals the actual number of visits in response to symptoms for a population segment and E represents the physicians' estimates of the number of visits that should have occurred. A minus score means fewer person sought care than the physicians judged necessary. A plus score indicates that a greater proportion sought care than the physicians thought necessary.

The symptoms-response ratio, as described above, was used as a measure of the utilization of services relative to need. Table 8-17 shows the symptoms-response ratio by race, age, and sex. The ratio for the entire sample was -13, which indicates that the total sample saw a physician less often than medically determined norms suggest they should have. Elderly whites and the young-old (aged 65-75) sought care at medically appropriate rates; however, elderly blacks, the old-old (over 76 years old), and males sought care significantly less often than medical norms suggest. Note that the race effect still obtains with age and sex controlled. And although females sought care in response to symptoms much more readily than did males, their responses were also inadequate.

Summary and Conclusions

Despite a higher level of morbidity, blacks average fewer visits to physicians per year than whites. During the 1970s blacks approached parity with whites in the raw mean number of visits per year. However, the decade of the eighties saw a widening of the gap between blacks and whites in visits to physicians.

Most of the race differentials in physician visits is accounted for by the black deficit in visits by individuals under 18 years of age. Above the age of 18 the rates are fairly equal, although females have more visits than males among both blacks and whites.

Low-income individuals have more physician visits among both blacks and whites than middle-income persons. Low-income persons also have longer stays when hospitalized, which suggests that their conditions are poorer when they enter the hospital. Whether low-income or not, blacks experience more days per hospital stay than whites.

Blacks make fewer visits to physicians' offices and more visits to hospital outpatient departments and emergency rooms, suggesting a lower quality of care. Blacks are also more dissatisfied with the medical care they receive.

One of the primary assurances of access to medical care is health insurance. Although Medicaid has been a major means of health insurance for poor persons, it does not cover all poor or low-income individuals. For example, less than 18% of blacks

Table 8-17

Symptoms-Response Ratio for Urban Elderly Sample, by Race, Age, and Sex

Characteristics	N	Actual Number of Visits for Symptoms (A)	Estimated Number of Visits for Symptoms (E)	Discrepancy Between Estimated & Actual Number Visits (A-E)	Symptoms-Response Ratio $\frac{(A-E)}{E} \times (100)$
Race					
White	839	1,278	1,309	-31	-2
Black	502	574	787	-213	-26[a]
Age					
65 - 75	879	1,267	1,289	-22	-1
Over 75	462	586	807	-221	-27[a]
Sex					
Male	455	433	575	-142	-25[a]
Female	886	1,419	1,521	-102	-7[a]
Total	1,341	1,852	2,096	-275	-13[a]

Note: Ratio for age is adjusted for sex, ratio for sex is adjusted for age, and ratio for race is adjusted for age and sex.

[a] $p \leqq .05$.

Source: Reed, W. (1984). *Access to Services by the Urban Elderly*. NTIS Pub. No. PB84-245364. Baltimore: Institute for Urban Research.

have Medicaid coverage. Another 57% have private insurance, and this rate is decreasing. All in all, nearly one in four blacks have no medical insurance.

In relation to health status blacks have fewer physician contacts per person than whites whether the comparison is made between those in poor health or good health. On the other hand, health status has no effect on the tendency of blacks to spend more days in the hospital per visit.

The black elderly have as many or more visits to physicians as the white elderly. Since the black elderly are at greater risk than the white elderly for acute as well as chronic diseases they should need more medical care. However, using a normed, need-based measure of access to medical care services we see the black elderly as underutilizers.

There are perhaps two primary factors involved in the underutilization of medical care by the black elderly. First, the general tendency to underutilize may be a function of the black elderly's experience with medical care services. Blacks tend to use public facilities and hospitals more readily than whites, and the concomitant result is a greater dissatisfaction with the care they receive. Secondly, many of the black elderly do not have supplementary (private) insurance to pay for visits to other places of care.

The data presented in this chapter indicate structural problems that impede the acquisition of requisite medical care among blacks. Economic differentials adversely affect the ability of blacks to carry private medical insurance, and Medicaid is covering a decreasing proportion of poor and low-income persons. In addition, a large proportion of blacks, as a result of economics and the associated medical care seeking behaviors, find themselves receiving a lower quality of medical care. A national health plan where medical care is provided to everyone–as it is in every other western democracy–would obviate most of these problems.

References

Aday, L., & Andersen, R. (1975). *Development of Indices of Access to Medical Care.* Ann Arbor, MI: Health Administration Press.

Aday, L., & Andersen, R. (1984). The National Profile of Access to Medical Care: Where Do We Stand? *American Journal of Public Health, 74* (12), 1331-39.

Andersen, R. (1978). Health Status Indices and Access to Medical Care. *American Journal of Public Health, 68* (5), 458-62.

Davis, K. (1976). Medical Payments and Utilization of Medical Services by the Room. *Inquiry, 13.*

Health Resources Administration. (1977). *Health of the Disadvantaged. Chartbook.* U.S. Department of Health, Education, and Welfare, Public Health Office, Office of Health Resources Opportunity. DHEW Pub. No. (HRA) 77-628. Washington, DC: U.S. Government Printing Office.

Link, C. R., Long, S. H., & Settle, R. F. (1982). Access to Medical Care Under Medicaid: Differentials by Race. *Journal of Health Politics and Law, 7* (2), 345-65.

National Center for Health Services Research. (1982). *Usual Sources of Medical Care and Their Characteristics.* Data Preview, 12. NCHSR National Health Care Expenditures Study. DHHS Pub. No. (PHS) 82-3324. Washington, DC: U.S. Government Printing Office.

National Center for Health Statistics. (1989). *The Nursing Home Survey: 1985 Summary for the United States.* Vital Health Statistics. Series 13, No. 97. DHHS Pub. No. (PHS) 89-1758. Public Health Services. Washington, DC: U.S. Government Printing Office.

National Center for Health Statistics. (1990). *Health, United States, 1989.* DHHS Pub. No. (PHS) 90-1232. Hyattsville, MD: Public Health Services.

Reed, W. L. (1984). *Access to Services by the Urban Elderly.* NTIS Pub. No. PB84-245364. Baltimore: Institute for Urban Research.

Reed, W. L. (1990). Health Care Needs and Services. In Z. Harel, E.A. McKinney, and M. Williams (Eds.), *Black Aged: Understanding Diversity and Service Needs.* Newbury Park, CA: Sage Publications.

Ries, P. W. (1990). *Health of Black and White Americans 1985-87.* National Center for Health Statistics. Vital Health Statistics. Series 10, No. 171. Public Health Service. Washington, DC: U.S. Government Printing Office.

Robert Wood Johnson Foundation. (1987). *Access to Health Care in the United States: Results of a 1986 Survey.* Princeton, NJ: Author.

Taylor, D. G., Aday, L. A. & Andersen, R. (1975). A Social Indicator of Access to Medical Care. *Journal of Health and Social Behavior, 16,* 38-49.

U.S. Department of Health and Human Services. (1985). *Report of the Secretary's Task Force on Black and Minority Health. Vol. 4, Cardiovascular and Cerebrovascular Disease.* Washington, DC: U.S. Government Printing Office.

9

Health Work Force Distribution

The black community has, because of restricted segregated housing, discrimination, and state and local segregation laws and practices, relied almost solely on black health personnel (pharmacists, dentists, nurses, physicians, public health specialists, allied health specialists, and so on) for service. Data show that there is a critical shortage in each of these specialty areas, with no sign of alleviation. If this shortage is to be remedied, then a major thrust must be made during the remainder of this century and well into the next to increase considerably the number of black Americans going into the health professions. This can only be carried out if a disproportionate recruitment effort is consciously made by education and health leaders at both the state and federal levels to correct historical inequities in education and health resources.

However, a dangerous and devious potential block to this goal and critical need is the so-called "glut of doctors" that was originally observed by President Jimmy Carter's Secretary of Health, Education, and Welfare, who called for a halt in the government's decade-old policy of encouraging medical schools to increase enrollments. The call was for reduced funding for health care personnel, beginning with drastic reductions in federal grants and funds for all health training. For instance, a featured article in the *New York Times* on December 3, 1978, indicated that President Carter's Office of Management and Budget was planning drastic cuts in health program financing. According to the article, "Documents indicate that the Budget Office is resolved to cut back sharply on many health programs. The working papers show, for example, that it would give no funds at all for comprehensive health grants to the states, now a $90 million-a-year preventive health program."

During the 1980s the Reagan administration continued this trend at a much more accelerated rate. Neither his administration nor Carter's pointed out, however, that the "glut" of health care personnel does not apply to the black community, the Mexican-American community, the native American community, or the mainland Puerto Rican community. As a result of this oversight, these ethnic minority communities have been caught in a drastic policy change regarding federal support for health professional education. The data reveal that African-Americans are the worst off of all ethnic minorities and that they are losing ground in the production of health professionals.

Health Professionals

The need for more African-American health professionals is clearly indicated in the following data. In reviewing the work force population ratios per 100,000 population for dentists, physicians, pharmacists, and nurses, it is evident that large disparities exist (see table 9-1). In 1975 there were 89.4 Asian dentists per 100,000 Asian population. This increased to 109.4 by 1980, for an increase of 22.4% during the five-year period. The rate for black Americans was 10.5 in 1975 and 12.0 in 1980, for an increase of 14.3%. For native Americans the rate was 8.3 per 100,000 native American population in 1975 and 13.4 in 1980, for an increase of 61.5%. For Hispanic Americans the rate was 11.3 Hispanic dentists per 100,000 Hispanic population in 1975 and 15.0 in 1980, for an increase of 32.7%; and for white Americans the rate was 50.1 in 1975 per 100,000 white population and 64.1 in 1980, for an increase of 27.9%.

The rate for pharmacists can also be seen in table 9-1. In 1975 there were 129.8 Asian pharmacists per 100,000 Asian population. This had increased to 187.9 by 1980, for an increase of 44.8%. For black Americans the rate for pharmacists was 12.3 per 100,000 black population in 1975. By 1980 the rate was 18.1 for an increase of 47.2%. For native Americans the rate was 16.6 in 1975; this had increased to 17.6 by 1980, for an increase of 6%. For Hispanics the rate was 23.1 in 1975 and 29.1 in 1980, for an increase of 26.0%. And for white Americans the rate was 60.0 in 1975 and 72.1 in 1980, for an increase of 20.2%.

In 1975, there were 731.2 Asian physicians per 100,000 Asian population, while in 1980, there were 1,197.4 for an increase of 63.8%. For black Americans these figures were 25.6 black physicians per 100,000 black population in 1975 and 50.7 in 1980, for an increase of 98%. For native Americans the number of physicians per 100,000 native American population in 1975 was 22.9 and in 1980 it was 36.0 for an increase of 57.2%. For the Hispanic population, the rate was 113.9 physicians per 100,000 Hispanic population in 1975, and 129.1 in 1980 for an increase of 13.3%. For white Americans the rate was 146.4 in 1975 and 198.7 in 1980, for an increase of 35.8%.

The rate for Asian registered nurses in 1975 was 788.6 per 100,000 Asian population and 1,226.8 in 1980 for an increase of 55.6%. For black Americans the rate was 289.2 per 100,000 population in 1975 and 365.4 in 1980 for an increase of 26.3%. For native Americans the rate in 1975 was 240.7 per 100,000 native American population and in 1980 it was 272.2 for an increase of 13.1%. For white Americans, the rate was 425.3 per 100,000 white population in 1975 and 616.0 in 1980, for an increase of 44.8%.

These data demonstrate that there is no glut among black health professionals: Black health professionals are less represented than any other group, except native Americans. Black physicians provide their services mainly to blacks. Thus the availability of black physicians must be considered in relation to the black population. This is a critical point, as some 87% of black physicians serve black patients and over 90% of nonblack physicians serve white patients when analyzed by ambulatory

Table 9-1

Work Force Rates per 100,000 Persons for Selected
Health Professions, by Race/Ethnicity, 1975 and 1980

Selected Professions	Rate by Race/Ethnicity				
	Black[a]	Hispanic	Native American	Asian	White[a]
Physicians					
1975	25.6	113.9	22.9	731.2	146.4
1980	50.7	129.1	36.0	1,197.4	198.7
Dentists					
1975	10.5	11.3	8.3	89.4	50.1
1980	12.0	15.0	13.4	109.4	64.1
Registered nurses					
1975	289.2	175.5	240.7	788.6	425.3
1980	365.4	188.6	272.2	1,226.8	616.0
Pharmacists					
1975	12.3	23.1	16.6	129.8	60.0
1980	18.1	29.1	17.6	187.9	72.1

[a]Excludes Hispanics.

Sources: U.S. Department of Health and Human Services. (1985). *Report of the Secretary's Task Force on Black and Minority Health. Vol. 2: Crosscutting Issues in Minority Health.* Washington, DC: U.S. Government Printing Office.

medical care patient visits (U.S. Department of Health and Human Services, 1982). In 1985 black physicians made up 3% of all physicians, or 15,600 out of a physician population of 520,700 (U.S. Department of Health and Human Services, 1990).

The so-called glut of physicians and other health personnel does not apply to the black population. The federal government's elimination of exceptional-need scholarships has already shown its effect on the black community in a significant decrease in black medical school enrollment, as well as in decreases in other health professional school enrollments. Given that the country's black population is served primarily by black physicians and health care workers, such decreases may be related to the increasing gap between blacks and whites in infant mortality rates, the incidence of malignant neoplasms, case rates of tuberculosis, and so on.

Blacks increased from 11.5% of the U.S. population in 1980 to an estimated 12.3% in 1987 (see table 9-2). However, blacks have continued to be underrepresented in health occupations (see table 9-3). In comparison to other minority groups, blacks are less represented in selected health occupations, considering their proportion of the overall population. During the period 1980 to 1987 blacks actually lost ground in producing selected health professionals. Although there was a small increase in the proportion of physicians who were black, the proportion of dentists who were black declined as did the proportion of black pharmacists. A more equitable share of registered nurses were black in 1980, and this share increased slightly in 1987.

Over the 20-year period from the 1968-69 academic year through the 1987-88 academic year, there were significant increases in the number and proportion of blacks graduating from schools for the health professions (see table 9-4). The greatest increase occurred in schools of medicine, where in 1968-69 only 1.8% of all graduates were black, but in 1987-88 5.5% were black, for an increase of over 300%. On the other hand, the proportion of physicians who are black would have to double again before it approaches representativeness; and, as we have seen, the rate of increase slowed considerably during the 1980s.

During the 1970s and 1980s black enrollments increased in dentistry, nursing, and pharmacy, with the smallest increase occurring in nursing (see table 9-5). Overall, the proportions of blacks enrolling in schools for the health professions are greater than the proportions of health practitioners who are black—as they would have to be if the proportion of health practitioners who are black is to increase. Relatively speaking, however, increases in enrollment rates, as well as in graduation rates, for other minority groups outpace those of blacks. This phenomenon is shown in table 9-6, which compares the parity indices across selected years for minority groups.

The parity index may be understood as follows: if among all first-year enrollees in a health profession school during a specific year, a minority group's proportion equaled that minority group's proportion in the overall population, the parity index would be 100. If the minority group's proportion was exactly one-half that of its proportion in the population, the parity index would be 50. Of the four minority groups

Table 9-2

Percentage Distribution of Population of the United States,
by Racial/Ethnic Category and Year

Race/Ethnicity	1970	1980	1987 (est.)
Black[a]	10.9%	11.5%	12.3%
Hispanic	4.5	6.4	7.5
Asian	0.8	1.5	–
Native American	0.4	0.6	–
White[a]	83.4	79.9	84.8

[a]Excludes Hispanics.

Source: U.S. Department of Health and Human Services. (1990, June). *Minorities and Women in the Health Fields.* Public Health Services. Health Resources and Services Administration. HRSA-P-DV 90-3. Washington, DC: U.S. Government Printing Office.

Table 9-3

Experienced Civilian Labor Force[a] in Selected Health Occupations,
by Racial/Ethnic Category, 1980 and 1987

Selected Occupations	Percent Distribution by Race/Ethnic Group				
	Black[b]	Hispanic	Native American	Asian	White[b]
Physicians					
1980	3.1%	4.4%	0.1%	9.7%	82.6%
1987	3.7	5.5	NA	NA	NA
Dentists					
1980	2.5	1.7	0.2	3.1	94.7
1987	2.1	3.3	NA	NA	NA
Registered nurses					
1980	7.4	2.1	0.3	3.3	86.7
1987	7.7	2.6	NA	NA	NA
Pharmacists					
1980	3.7	2.4	0.2	4.5	89.6
1987	3.0	1.9	NA	NA	NA

[a]The 1980 data include civilian persons employed in 1980 or unemployed having civilian experience between 1975 and 1980. The 1987 data includes only employed civilian workers.
[b]Excludes Hispanics.

NA = Not available.

Source: U.S. Department of Health and Human Services. (1990, June). *Minorities and Women in the Health Fields*. Public Health Services. Health Resources and Services Administration. HRSA-P-DV 90-3. Washington, DC: U.S. Government Printing Office.

Table 9-4

Graduates of Schools of Selected Health Professions,
by Racial/Ethnic Category, Recent Years

Selected Professional Schools	Percent Distribution by Race/Ethnicity				
	Black	Hispanic	Native American	Asian	White
Medicine					
1968-69	1.8%	NA	NA	NA	NA
1978-79	5.2	2.2%	0.3%	2.3%	89.9%
1987-88	5.5	3.8	0.4	7.2	83.2
Dentistry					
1971-72	1.9	0.3	NA	1.6	95.7
1978-79	3.4	1.4	0.3	3.9	91.0
1987-88	5.0	4.9	0.3	10.2	81.0
Nursing					
1971-72	5.5	1.5	NA	NA	NA
1977-78	4.7	2.3	NA	NA	NA
1987-88	8.3	2.9	NA	NA	NA
Pharmacy					
1971-72	2.9	3.2	NA	NA	91.4
1978-79	3.7	3.9	0.2	3.6	88.3
1986-87	5.4	4.7	0.1	6.7	82.7

NA = Not available.

Source: U.S. Department of Health and Human Services. (1990, June). *Minorities and Women in the Health Fields*. Public Health Services. Health Resources and Services Administration. HRSA-P-DV 90-3. Washington, DC: U.S. Government Printing Office.

Table 9-5

First-Year Enrollment for Selected Health Professions,
by Race/Ethnic Category, Recent Years

Selected Professions	Percent Distribution by Racial/Ethnic Category			
	Black	Hispanic	Native American	Asian
Medicine				
1971-72	7.1%	1.3%	0.2%	1.8%
1978-79	6.4	4.0	0.3	2.7
1988-89	7.2	5.6	0.45	12.4
Dentistry				
1971-72	5.2	0.9	0.09	2.4
1978-79	4.5	2.0	0.26	4.2
1988-89	6.9	7.6	0.50	16.4
Nursing				
1971-72	7.7	2.0	NA	NA
1977-78	7.2	2.5	NA	NA
1984-85	8.0	2.5	NA	NA
Pharmacy				
1973-74	3.3	1.6	0.12	3.0
1978-79	4.3	1.9	0.14	3.8
1987-88	6.0	3.7	0.22	7.0

NA = Not ascertained.

Source: U.S. Department of Health and Human Services. (1990, June). *Minorities and Women in the Health Fields.* Public Health Services. Health Resources and Services Administration. HRSA-P-DV 90-3. Washington, DC: U.S. Government Printing Office.

Table 9-6

Parity Index[a] for Enrollment in Selected Health Professional Schools,
by Race/Ethnicity, Recent Years

Selected Professions	Black	Hispanic	Native American	Asian
Medicine				
1971-72	65	28	44	222
1978-79	56	67	51	201
1984-85	57	72	61	321
1988-89	60	64	51	454
Dentistry				
1971-72	47	20	21	296
1978-79	39	33	46	313
1984-85	51	53	46	452
1988-89	57	87	57	601
Nursing				
1971-72	70	43	NA	NA
1977-78	64	43	NA	NA
1984-85	68	33	NA	NA
Pharmacy				
1973-74	30	32	26	319
1978-79	38	32	25	284
1984-85	54	39	22	282
1987-88	50	45	26	275

[a]Parity Index = Percent of first year enrollment divided by percent of total
 population times 100.
NA = Not ascertained.

Source: U.S. Department of Health and Human Services. (1990, June). *Minorities and Women in the Health Fields*. Public Health Services. Health Resources and Services Administration. HRSA-P-DV 90-3. Washington, DC: U.S. Government Printing Office.

presented in table 9-6, only Asians had greater than parity participation. Their enrollment rates greatly exceed their proportions in the population.

In table 9-6 we see that blacks have been losing ground in enrollment in schools of medicine: the parity index was lower in 1989-89 than it was in 1971-72. On the other hand, the parity indices for enrollment in schools of medicine increased significantly for the other minority groups. The parity index increased slightly for black enrollment in dental schools, while at the same time there were substantial increases for the other minority groups. Blacks held somewhat steady in enrollment in schools of nursing, while the rate for Hispanics fell between 1971-72 and 1984-85. And blacks as well as Hispanics had increased parity rates for entering pharmacy schools.

Overall, for these selected health professions blacks experienced increased enrollment; however, because in several instances they failed to keep pace with their rate of population increase, it is more accurate to conclude that blacks have actually lost ground in the realm of the health professional work force.

Unmet Health Care Needs

The combination of poverty, unemployment, low levels of education, and substandard housing has created a permanently underserved population within a disproportionately large number of black communities in the nation. These interrelated factors are all associated with poor health status, as is reflected elsewhere in this volume. A greater prevalence of disease in association with other indices of social disorganization in these underserved communities leaves this population particularly vulnerable to health financing arrangements that promote the idea that "less care is better." It is very clear that this population needs more medical care as well as some alleviation of the conditions that produce poor health; and it is also clear that measures requisite to the removal of health status deficits are not without cost.

Between 1980 and 1986 the number and proportion of persons below the poverty level increased slightly. At the same time the proportion of persons covered by Medicaid decreased and the proportion of individuals not covered by any health insurance increased from 12.5% to 15.3%. Additionally, persons earning less than $10,000 a year and not insured increased by 16% (U.S. Department of Health and Human Services, 1990).

These trends strongly suggest an increasing need for "free" care. However, during the early 1980s, the observed volume of free care increased only slightly. Most private hospitals provided relatively little free care despite relatively strong financial pictures. Public hospitals in metropolitan areas (the nation's one hundred largest cities) did expand their efforts in providing free care, but the limited availability of resources constrained an actual expansion in the volume of free care. In nonmetropolitan and rural areas the amount of free care provided by both public and private hospitals actually decreased from 1980 to 1982 (American Hospital Association and the Urban Institute, 1984). Although one might argue that those individuals newly entering poverty were in need of less care than those for whom poverty had been long-standing, and, therefore, that new poverty entrants did not increase the demand for care, most data suggest that less care means poorer health.

Observations of increased poverty and inadequate insurance in the face of a relatively small increase in the free care provided by hospitals is particularly relevant to black communities. Black Americans have been disproportionately represented among the poor, the unemployed, and the uninsured. In 1980, 32.5% of the black population was living in poverty, compared with 10.2% of white Americans (U.S. Department of Health and Human Services, 1990). In 1986, among persons less than 65 years of age, 79.1% of white Americans had private insurance; while only 57% of black Americans had private insurance. Over 17% (17.4) of black Americans in the below-65 age group were insured by Medicaid and 22.6% had no health insurance (U.S. Department of Health and Human Services, 1990). Consequently, current trends that limit public health care funding disproportionately affect black Americans.

Hospitals have been a major source of health care for black Americans. The absence of physicians' offices in underserved communities has been well-documented (Davis, 1978; Reed, 1980; Riessman, 1981). Because black Americans are more likely to receive physician visits in hospital clinics or emergency rooms than white Americans, blacks are more likely to be affected by trends in the availability of hospital services. Additionally, black Americans are twice as likely as white Americans to receive physicians' services in schools, places of employment, and public health clinics; therefore, the vulnerability of black Americans to decreases in publicly supported health programs is increased (Donabedian, Axelrod, & Wyszewianski, 1980).

Hospitals have traditionally rationed free care by using two strategies: explicitly discouraging or prohibiting hospital use by people unable to pay; and reducing the availability of services heavily used by the uninsured poor. Although these strategies are enforced to differing degrees, they limit both access to and the availability of certain services. Emergency services are usually protected by ethical and medicolegal constraints. Non-emergency and preventive care are often the first services to be limited. In view of the association of the receipt of prenatal care and preventive services with the lowering of infant mortality rates, careful attention should be given to any policies that could provide hospitals with additional incentives to limit access to free care or inadequately reimbursed services.

Health Professional Availability

The availability of health services is positively correlated with the supply of health professionals. The Graduate Medical Education National Advisory Committee projected a surplus of physicians by 1990. Even if such a surplus has been attained, the supply of black physicians, dentists, and pharmacists is still inadequate. In 1980 there was 1 black physician (M.D.s and D.O.s) for every 2,264 black persons in the population, compared with 1 physician for every 647 persons in the general population. The disparity in these ratios for dentistry and pharmacy is even more striking, with 1 black dentist for every 7,297 black persons in the population and 1 black pharmacist for every 7,838 black persons, as compared with ratios for the general population of 1:1,795 and 1:1,571 for dentistry and pharmacy, respectively (U.S. Department of Health and Human Services, 1982). Because 87% of black physicians serve black patients and 90.4% of nonblack physicians serve the white population, the disparity in ratios reflects a disparity in the availability at least of services.

While one must applaud the increase in the *numbers* of black health professionals during the 1970s, this increase has fallen far short of goals to bring parity in the representation and availability of black health professionals. Furthermore, new uncertainties about medicine as a career choice, given the projected surplus of physicians and the fact of rising indebtedness among medical students, has already resulted in a decline in the medical school applicant pool. As U.S. medical schools respond to these changes by gradually decreasing first year enrollment, we cannot expect to see a significant increase in black first-year enrollment in the absence of constructive intervention.

Health Services Reorganization

Uncertainties about the financing of health care services have catalyzed changes in traditional organizational relationships in the health industry. While on one hand some of these developments offer the promise of rationalizing the health care system, they provide little encouragement that those individuals who are currently underserved will reap any benefit. Whether the organizational framework be a health maintenance organization (HMO), preferred provider organization (PPO), or investor-owned health system, the measure of success will be viewed in terms of the ability of the organization to provide the same or less care at a lower cost. In such a scenario those individuals with substantial health care needs become liabilities unless government intervention provides a sufficiently strong "safety net."

If the differential ratios in health care between black and white Americans are to be reduced, government must provide the vehicle to ensure equal access and stimulate the equal availability of services in the current system of health care. In an environment in which savings–whether distributed to the employer, the employee, the stockholder, or all three–will be rewarded, there must be reward for providing the preventive, diagnostic, and treatment services needed to decrease differential deficit ratios existing in many communities.

Summary and Conclusions

Sustaining health care to the underinsured is a long-term, not transitory problem. Expanding health insurance or subsidizing health facilities are the two general approaches to solving the problem. To become reality, however, a specific solution must not only maintain access, but should do so efficiently. Fear of exacerbating a medical cost escalation that is already considered out of control has, of course, become a major obstacle to expanding public health insurance. During the 1980s national health insurance disappeared from the policy agenda: incremental improvements in public programs–health insurance for the unemployed–failed to pass Congress; and preexisting benefits in Medicare and Medicaid have been cut back. However, the growing costs of medical care and medical insurance have brought about renewed discussions in Congress about a national health insurance plan.

It is not realistic to think that we can make significant strides in reducing inequities in health status if the burden rests solely on local governments. The inequities of local contributions to Medicaid across the nation would serve as a lesson in the future. The most equitable way to raise funds to support programs targeted to decrease differential deficit ratios in health care is from general tax revenues. In the absence of a more comprehensive health system or health insurance plan, funds can be raised by taxing net revenues of hospitals that do not serve the underserved and taxing insurance premiums to support institutions that develop programs to meet the needs of the underserved.

Closing the gap in the training of black health professionals first requires recognition that the problem exists. Public awareness must be increased. Most communications address a projected physician surplus, few note the inadequacy in the numbers of black physicians. It is the public awareness of a projected surplus that supports decreases in financial support for the recruitment and training of health professionals.

Given the increasing indebtedness among medical students, incentives to practice in underserved areas can and should be provided through loan forgiveness programs. Such programs can stimulate commitments to needed primary care specialities and increase the availability of physicians in black communities.

There is strong evidence that the health status of black Americans continues to be far below that of white Americans. The combination of inequities in income, employment, and access to and the availability of health care services, together with the fact that we have a health care industry which encourage competition, only promises to erode past progress and widen racial differences if direct government intervention is not forthcoming.

References

American Hospital Association and the Urban Institute. (1984). *1980-82 Survey of Medical Care for the Poor and Hospitals' Financing Status.* Washington, DC: The Urban Institute.

Davis, J. W. (1978). Decentralization, Citizen Participation, and Ghetto Health Care. In H. D. Schwartz and C. S. Kart, *Dominant Issues in Medical Sociology.* Reading, MA: Addison-Wesley.

Donabedian, A., Axelrod, S. J., and Wyszewianski, L. (1980). *Medical Care Chartbook.* Ann Arbor, MI: Health Administration Press.

Reed, W. L. (1980). Access to Services by Urban Target Populations. *Massachusetts Journal of Community Health, 1* (3), 9-17.

Riessman, C. K. (1981). Improving the Use of Health Services by the Poor. In P. Conrad and R. Kern (Eds.), *Critical Perspectives in the Sociology of Health and Illness* (2nd ed.). New York: St. Martin's Press.

U.S. Department of Health and Human Services. (1985). *Report of the Secretary's Task Force on Black and Minority Health. Vol. 2: Crosscutting Issues in Minority Health.* Washington, DC: U.S. Government Printing Office.

U.S. Department of Health and Human Services. (1982, September). *Estimates and Projections of Black and Hispanic Personnel in Selected Health Professions 1980-2000.* Washington, DC: U.S. Government Printing Office.

U.S. Department of Health and Human Services. (1990). *Health Status of the Disadvantaged–Chartbook 1990.* DHHS Pub. No. (HRSA) HRS-P-DV 90-1. Washington, DC: U.S. Government Printing Office.

U.S. Department of Health and Human Services. (1990, June). *Minorities and Women in the Health Fields.* Public Health Service. Health Resources and Service Administration. HRSA-P-DV 90-3. Washington, DC: U.S. Government Printing Office.

10

Cross-Cutting Issues in the Health
of African-Americans

African-Americans are represented in every socioeconomic group in the country; however, one-third live in poverty, a rate three times that of white Americans. Although they live in all regions of the country, more than one-half of African-Americans live in central cities, in areas typified by poverty, poor schools, crowded housing, unemployment, violence, and high levels of stress. The effects of racial disadvantages that African-Americans suffer are nowhere more telling and more significant than in mortality rates and life expectancy. Blacks simply do not live as long as whites. Life expectancy for blacks has perennially lagged behind that of whites, and in recent years the situation has appeared to worsen. Since the mid-1980s the gap has widened, with life expectancy increasing to 75 years for the overall population, and falling from a high of 69.7 years in 1984 to 69.4 years in 1987 for African-Americans (U.S. Department of Health and Human Services, 1991).

The leading chronic diseases causing death among blacks are the same as those for the white population, but the rates among blacks are consistently greater, often much greater. For example, black men die from strokes at almost twice the rate of all men in the total population, and they also have higher rates of nonfatal strokes (U.S. Department of Health and Human Services, 1991).

Black men also have a higher risk of cancer than other men–25% higher for all cancers and 45% higher for lung cancer. And only 38% of blacks with cancer survive five years after diagnosis, compared to 50% of whites. Diabetes is one-third more prevalent among blacks than among whites, and the complications of diabetes–heart disease, stroke, kidney failure, and blindness–all are more prevalent among blacks with diabetes than whites with diabetes.

Black babies are twice as likely as white babies to die before their first birthday. High rates of low birth weight among black babies account for a large proportion of these excess deaths; however, even normal-weight black babies have a greater risk of death. Homicide is the most frequent cause of death for black men between the ages of 15 and 34, with a rate that is seven times that of whites. A black man has a 1-in-21 lifetime chance of being murdered, and black women are more than four times as likely to be homicide victims as white women. Homicide and infant mortality are significant factors in the gap in life expectancy of blacks and whites.

The rate of AIDS among blacks is more than triple that of whites. The gaps are even greater among women and children, with black women having some 10 to 15 times the risk of AIDS as white women and black children accounting for more than 50% of all children with AIDS.

Among other disparities in health risks for African-Americans, hypertension stands out. High blood pressure is much more prevalent among blacks than among whites. Black men have severe high blood pressure at four times the rate of white men. Overweight–a risk factor for high blood pressure–occurs more often among black women than white women.

In assessing the health status of African-Americans it is important to note the persistence of sickle cell anemia as a major health problem. One out of every 400 black babies is born with sickle cell anemia, an incurable disease that predicts shorter life spans and life-long problems of pain and illness. Notably, sickle cell anemia occurs six times more often in blacks than does diabetes in the general population. Yet it does not get the attention as a societal problem that such prevalence would suggest.

Lead poisoning is a problem that affects more than 50% of black urban children. While only a small proportion of this number have the level of lead intoxication that causes illness, the vast majority suffer some level of irreversible neurological damage, which is increasingly being seen as a factor in school achievement and behavior. The Secretary of Health and Human Services estimates that "As many as three to four million of (all) children under 6 years of age–17% of that age group–may have blood levels high enough to cause mental and behavioral problems and other adverse health effects" (Murphy, 1991, p. 1). Some of the results of lead exposure include decreased intelligence, developmental delays, behavioral disturbances, decreased stature, and anemia (Murphy, 1991).

Adolescent pregnancy is a major concern for African-Americans for social and economic reasons as well as for health reasons. First, for young mothers there is increased risk of low birth weight babies and infant death. But perhaps more significant is the potential for low educational attainment and lives of poverty–and the problems these entail–for the mother and the baby.

Blacks do not receive enough early, routine, and preventive health care. Early prenatal care can reduce low birth weight and prevent infant deaths. Early detection of cancers can increase survival rates, and appropriate medical care can reduce the severity of diabetes. However, blacks do not obtain this level of medical care. Moreover, in comparison to need for care, blacks seek care less often than they should.

Six primary causes account for over 80% of the excess deaths among black males and females below age 70. The "excess deaths" index expresses the foregoing and presents evidence of the important part that socioeconomic status plays in the excess morbidity and mortality of African-Americans. However, if socioeconomic effects are controlled, great health disparities still exist between blacks and whites. Some differences in health are not explained solely by poverty (U. S. Department of Health and Human Services, 1991). In the Otten, et al (1991) study (referred to above) socioeconomic status (SES) only accounted for 38% of the black-white differences in mortality. And in Chapter 2 blacks are shown to have excess infant mortality beyond that explained by SES. These data suggest very strongly that aspects of the social situation (i.e., stress, physical environment) affect many African-Americans regardless of SES.

Reducing Mortality and Morbidity

We must continue to improve health care delivery for African-Americans. However, more health care alone will not solve all of their health problems. It is often assumed that improving access to medical care will eliminate the disparities in health status, but the effect of medical care is small when compared to non-medical variables. Studies have shown that medical care can explain no more than 10% of the variation in health status (Williams, 1990; U.S. Department of Health, Education, and Welfare, 1979). Some scholars argue that greater reductions in morbidity and mortality are more possible through additional expenditures on education than additional expenditures on medical care (Williams, 1991).

For some of the more prevalent chronic diseases the prescriptions for prevention and reduction are changes in lifestyle, changes such as diet, exercise, and the avoidance of alcohol and tobacco. This approach turns the attention to individual health behaviors. Individual health behaviors such as the use of tobacco and alcohol are important determinants of health condition. Almost half of the U.S. mortality is attributable to unhealthy behaviors or lifestyle (U.S. Department of Health and Welfare, 1979). For example, cigarette smoking and/or alcohol abuse are risk factors for five of the six causes of death discussed above (Williams, 1991).

Health behaviors, however, are not matters of personal choice only, as there is a social distribution of health behaviors. Health behaviors are affected by the social structure. Alcohol and tobacco use are socially accepted ways of getting relief from working and/or living conditions. Cigarette smoking as well as alcohol use increases during periods of high stress (or distress) (Williams, 1991). Of course, this is not to say that all or most of the use of tobacco or alcohol serve these "relief" purposes. Rather, we wish to show the connection that studies have established in this regard.

A perennial lament of leaders in central city communities is the heavy concentration of billboards for alcohol and tobacco products and the saturation of these communities with liquor stores. Smoking and alcohol are directly related to over one-half million deaths a year in the United States; and black communities suffer disproportionately. The relatively low price and the ready availability of these products are the result of actions by the state in cooperation with the alcohol and tobacco interests (Williams, 1979). The dependence of the state on the tobacco and alcohol revenues and the influence of the powerful economic interests prevent any adverse regulation of these businesses, overriding public health interests.

Improvement in the health of African-Americans requires a multipronged effort. There is a need to improve access to medical care for African-Americans. This includes providing for the availability of medical care services as well as the provision of such services to low-income persons without the usual stigma that many of them feel when they visit medical care facilities. Both issues could be handled if the United States instituted a universal health care plan, a situation that exists in every other western industrialized country except South Africa.

As suggested above, however, medical care, will not reduce completely the great disparities in health status between black and white Americans. To address such remaining disparities we must work on other aspects of society. We must understand that disease is rooted in the social structure; and we must understand and address the means by which the social structure affects the distribution of healthy as well as unhealthy behaviors.

References

Murphy, J. (1991, May-June). Federal Agencies Gearing Up for New Efforts Against Lead. *The Nation's Health*. P. 1.

U. S. Department of Health and Human Services. (1991). *Healthy People: National Health Promotion and Disease Prevention Objectives*. Washington, DC: U.S. Government Printing Office.

U.S. Department of Health and Welfare. (1979). *Healthy People: The Surgeon General's Report on Health Promotion and Disease Prevention*. Washington, DC: U.S. Department of Health and Welfare.

Williams, R. (1990). Social Structure and the Health Status of Black Males. *Challenge*.

APPENDIX

Assessment of the Status of African-Americans
Project Study Group Members

Project Leaders

Director: Wornie L. Reed, William Monroe Trotter Institute, University of Massachusetts at Boston, 1985-1991 (since August 1991, Urban Child Research Center, Cleveland State University)

Co-Chair: James E. Blackwell, Department of Sociology, University of Massachusetts at Boston

Co-Chair: Lucius J. Barker, Department of Political Science, Washington University

Study Group on Education

Charles V. Willie (Chair), School of Education, Harvard University
Antoine M. Garibaldi (Vice-Chair), Dean, College of Arts and Science, Xavier University
Robert A. Dentler, Department of Sociology, University of Massachusetts at Boston
Robert C. Johnson, Minority Studies Academic Program, St. Cloud State University
Meyer Weinberg, Department of Education, University of Massachusetts at Amherst

Study Group on Employment, Income and Occupations

William Darity, Jr., (Chair) Department of Economics, University of North Carolina
Barbara Jones (Vice-Chair), College of Business, Prairie View A&M University
Jeremiah P. Cotton, Department of Economics, University of Massachusetts at Boston
Herbert Hill, Industrial Relations Research Institute, University of Wisconsin

Study Group on Political Participation and
the Administration of Justice

Michael B. Preston (Chair), Department of Political Science, University of Southern California
Diane M. Pinderhughes (Vice-Chair), Department of Political Science, University of Illinois/Champaign

Tobe Johnson, Department of Political Science, Morehouse College
Nolan Jones, Committee on Criminal Justice and Public Protection,
       National Governors Association
Susan Welch, Department of Political Science, University of Nebraska
John Zipp, Department of Sociology, University of Wisconsin at Milwaukee

Study Group on Social and Cultural Change

Alphonso Pinkney (Chair), Department of Sociology, Hunter College
James Turner (Vice-Chair), Africana Studies and Research Center, Cornell
       University
John Henrik Clarke, Professor Emeritus, Department of Black and Puerto Rican
       Studies, Hunter College
Sidney Wilhelm, Department of Sociology, State University of New York-Buffalo

Study Group on Health Status and Medical Care

William Darity, Sr. (Chair), School of Public Health, University of Massachusetts
       at Amherst
Stanford Roman (Vice-Chair), Morehouse School of Medicine, Atlanta
Claudia Baquet, National Cancer Institute, Bethesda, Maryland
Noma L. Roberson, Department of Cancer Control and Epidemiology, Rockwell Park
       Institute

Study Group on the Family

Robert B. Hill (Chair), Institute for Urban Research, Morgan State University
Andrew Billingsley (Vice-Chair), Department of Family and Community
       Development, University of Maryland
Eleanor Engram, Engram-Miller Associates, Cleveland, Ohio
Michelene R. Malson, Department of Public Policy Studies, Duke University
Roger H. Rubin, Department of Family and Community Development, University of
       Maryland
Carol B. Stack, Social and Cultural Studies, Graduate School of Education,
       University of California at Berkeley
James B. Stewart, Black Studies Program, Pennsylvania State University
James E. Teele, Department of Sociology, Boston University

Contributors

Carolyne Arnold, College of Public and Community Services, University of Massachusetts at Boston

James Banks, School of Education, University of Washington

Margaret Beale Spencer, College of Education, Emory University

Bob Blauner, Department of Sociology, University of California, Berkeley

Larry Carter, Department of Sociology, University of Oregon

Obie Clayton, School of Criminal Justice, University of Nebraska

James P. Comer, Department of Psychiatry, Yale Medical School

Charles Flowers, Department of Education, Fisk University

Bennett Harrison, Urban Studies and Planning, Massachusetts Institute of Technology

Norris M. Haynes, Child Study Center, New Haven

Joseph Himes, Excellence Fund Professor Emeritus of Sociology, University of North Carolina at Greensboro

Hubert E. Jones, School of Social Work, Boston University

James M. Jones, Department of Psychology, University of Delaware

Faustine C. Jones-Wilson, *Journal of Negro Education*, Howard University

Barry A. Krisberg, National Council on Crime and Delinquency, San Francisco

Hubert G. Locke, Society of Justice Program, University of Washington

E. Yvonne Moss, William Monroe Trotter Institute, University of Massachusetts at Boston

Willie Pearson, Jr., Department of Sociology, Wake Forest University

Michael L. Radelet, Department of Sociology, University of Florida

Robert Rothman, *Education Week*, Washington, DC

Diana T. Slaughter, School of Education, Northwestern University

A. Wade Smith, Department of Sociology, Arizona State University

Leonard Stevens, Compact for Educational Opportunity, Milwaukee

Wilbur Watson, Geriatrics Department, Morehouse School of Medicine

Warren Whatley, Department of Economics, University of Michigan

John B. Williams, Graduate School of Education, Harvard University

Rhonda Williams, Afro-American Studies, University of Maryland

Reginald Wilson, American Council of Education, Washington, DC